INTANGIBLE INTIMACY

THE DIARY OF A KING DAVID ADMIRER

SHALOM J. STEWART

Intangible Intimacy: The Diary of a King David Admirer

1. Spirituality 2. Self Help 3. Christianity 4. Religion 5. Inspirational

Printed in the United States

Contents

This book is dedicated first back to my best friend, the Holy Ghost. Also to my wife, Hana; my mother, Gail; and my sister, Shira. I love you all and you each challenge me to be the best man I can be in God. Thank you for never allowing me to come short of who God is calling me to be.

I Love Y'all!

~ Chapter One ~

PEOPLE IN PROPORTIONS

The Layers of Character

As I mature as a person and in my patience with people, I've come to find that the characters of people are designed by God with layers. These layers of character include one's image, identity, and integrity. Character is a major factor that has been down played in society. This is especially true in American society. What ever happened to manners and dignity and honor and humility? I could go on and on, but in essence, human character in the right standard has been corrupted because people have chosen to disregard its importance for the benefit of comfort.

In the world as well as the church, this is an issue. No one wants to take responsibility that they are somebody. We say we have value. We say we are priceless. We say we are educated. We even say we are children of God. Yet these sayings have become nothing more but labels of false identity in society as we neglect accepting who we truly are. It really all comes down to holding to one's integrity. Our integrity is the core root of our character. It's the essential foundation of who we are; our standards. We often abandon our integrity in certain moments in life because we lack discipline in ourselves as we don't exercise self-control for our neighbor's welfare.

Every person on this Earth is responsible for portraying and maintaining good character as God intended. Each individual in time has a chronicle as each person has an origin that proceeds them, a story that we live out, and a legacy that we leave behind after we die. Every story must have characters to play out their roles in the plot of the chronicles of life.

People are spirits with bodies that were created in a similar structure as the world we inhabit. Human beings have layers just as the Earth has layers; which consist of the crust, mantle, and core. The layers of people are fractions that consist of our physical, mental, and spiritual being. The physical being (our crust) would be our image. The mental being (our mantle) would be our identity. The spiritual being (our core) would be our integrity. The deeper we dig into people the more in depth we find the essential nature of a person down to their core- the intangible part of who they are. This is the part of us that truly matters.

Image: Handling Tangible Me Intangibly

Our image represents the outer most layer of our identity. It is the most tangible portion of our character that is more subject to the constraints of time than any other layer. Image is the only part of us that is irrelevant to eternity as it is the part of us that represents our character in a physical way.

The ideal of our image layer is materialistic. By this I mean that image is mostly based upon physical outlook. It is the part of our character that is most susceptible to tangibility and is the most liable to the laws of nature. Our image is the part of us that plays a major role against living life intangibly.

Today, people are more materialistic than ever before. We put more emphasis on image than any other part of character. It amazes me how people place most of their focus on the weakest portion of human character. Because image is tangible, it is the most vulnerable part of us. Our image is the shell of our spirit and is the easiest to harm. Yet it is the toughest to break because of it's flexibility and instinct to conform. It is the layer of our character that comes with many layers and has the ability to adjust.

We adjust our image based on different circumstances we may face in life. This layer of our character is the portion of us that shows how corrupt we really are. However, it is not the source of our character's corruption more than it is the result of corrupted character. As we look at the images of others we become corrupt and place their portrayal of image upon our own. This is how sin takes root and we become corrupt.

We are fearfully and wonderfully made as God has designed us from the inner core root of our integrity to the outer crust of our image. By this we can know that God has made every portion of us all unique despite how similar we may look to another. Consider twins! Twins may look very much alike, but even their fingerprints are different, their ability academically, and their own perspective on morals and values, may vary. So you see, we are all unique in every portion of who we are.

When placing someone else's portrayal of image upon our own we corrupt ourselves and defile God's original authentic design of who we are. However, this is a common tangible habit people display. So how do I handle the tangible portion of my character intangibly?

Well for starters, we have to understand that we literally can't do anything without God. There is no part of us that can exist without God. Every bit of who we are, tangible and intangible, belongs to God and is completely void without him. "In God we live and in God we die," literally. Our lives, our very existence is that deep in God. God is the source and resource of all things. Without God nothing can operate.

Knowing this is the first step in bringing our image into subjection. Our image must become subject to our identity and our identity must become subject to our integrity. In order for us to look right in the sight of God physically we have to be right in the sight of God on the inside spiritually and mentally. Some of us who are not right on the inside are too naive. We are so much into ourselves and others that feed our own self view of who we want to be. I wonder have we really ever considered how WE relate to one another?

I pose this question to bring to the light that we must get into the habit of examining ourselves daily. "Let a man examine himself!" If I am a representative of God, I ought to make sure that the image that is representing God on the outside is matching up with the image of God on the inside. If my identity is not identical with Christ I need work in me. If my integrity is not built on the foundation of Christ I need work in me. How many of us are standing before the people of God to bring them into a place of wholeness and freedom on one accord with God, but we are not whole and free within our own selves?

The problem that I see God is not pleased with is that the world and the church seem to be starting to unify in image. This raises some uneasiness because the world serves one master and the church serves another. This brings automatic division.

The church has allowed too much worldly methods, motives, and mentalities into its four walls and this is what causes the division. Remember "A house divided against its self shall not stand". Not to be deep, but the Bible used for example a "house" and not a "world". So I'm suggesting that the house of God on Earth has been breached with a worldly spirit and now division is starting to take form causing us to fall apart.

The Bible refers to our body as the Temple that "houses" the Holy Spirit. If my personal house (my being) is divided against itself on the inside (my identity and integrity) then the image of my personal house is in jeopardy of falling. In order for us to get a handle on our tangible selves we must first get an intangible grip on the Holy Spirit. We do this by conforming to the identity and integrity of Jesus Christ so we can live a tangible life based upon intangible standards. We do this by studying God's Word.

The first step in achieving this is identifying who we are in Jesus Christ because it is "in him that we live, move, and have our being." It is through Christ that the tangible and intangible meet and can operate on one accord. "It is all about the Spirit." This is a tip that my mother used to always say to my sister and I that helped me understand the importance of this topic regarding character once I became a mature Christian.

I have learned that I cannot get on one accord with myself mentally because my spirit and my body will constantly be at war against each other. It is better to get on one accord with Jesus Christ so that we can be on one accord with our Father in Heaven. This way all our hearts, minds, and souls will operate in the same direction no matter what level of knowledge, amount of skill, etcetera. It really doesn't matter too much to God, just get on one accord with Him by "seeking first the Kingdom of God and all its righteousness then all things shall be added." You do the possible things you can do and God will do the impossible and possible things we cannot do.

Identity: Refining Character

Identity is another layer of character that is a deeper part of us that is intangible but has the most direct effect on our layer of image. Just to pick our brains philosophically, image shows what we look like, identity is why we look the way we look, integrity is how we arrive to why we look the way we look. This leads us to what we look like. Our identity is an essential part of us that makes us unique because identity is who we are individually.

As we continue to live, our identity goes through changes because we experience different things in life as we grow. Growth naturally and spiritually develops us. Some general things about who we are will remain the same, but most things will change. It's all about adapting to life so that we can survive and move forward to progress.

I have learned that in order to know and be confident in one's true identity, one must be refined and not defined. More importantly, we must know who we are in Christ. Knowing who we are in Christ contributes more to our integrity but this is what helps us to not violate or defile our entire character. "To your own self be true!" If we don't have an idea of who we are in Christ anyone can tell us who we are and be effective. Now most people, especially people in their immature youth or pride, may disagree, but I find that if I am not secure in whom I am, or confident in who I can be, I can easily be persuaded about my identity.

Anytime we can be persuaded against whom we are, this shows that there is insecurity because we lack assurance in who we are. There could be plenty of reasons why this may not be totally our fault but it is still a vulnerable state for us to be in. A good way to become secure and confident about whom we are is by being secure and confident about who we cannot be. In God's Word we are told of everything we are, are not, should, and should not be. If we seek God to know who He is He will show us who we are. People fail to seek God and meditate on His Word by not studying His Word. As a result, people fail to gain understanding by default.

God tells us who we are and who we are not in His Word because we are His children. God will not allow His children to walk around not knowing who they are. How can God make effective use of us to draw the lost if we are lost ourselves? If God is not using us are we His children or the enemy? Whoever is using us is our actual father. We should consider who we identify with the most.

There is only one way to live right and get into the Kingdom of Heaven and that way is Jesus Christ. Christ makes the difference in our identity of character, and Christ is the example we have to identify with God's character. Christ is the equalizer of our identity that refines who we are. No matter where you've been, what you've done, who you were, etcetera, Christ is the equalizer and is the one who causes us to change from the inside out, making us new creatures. Christ refines us but this is a process that is continual throughout our lives.

Our identity must be christened, purged in refinement. Christening our identity is a spiritual process I find to be baptism by fire. It takes longer than the physical baptism we normally do which is a public display of our claim to Christ. This process is a spiritual purification: A process of submerging the old in spiritual fire to purify and cleanse.

Some people are refined in character through tough situations. It all depends on what the individual needs to go through in God and it is all up to God. There are "different strokes for different folks", and God has to whip some of us into shape for Him for a long period of time. God does this so that we can reach an agreement with the mindset that "We are God's and God is ours."

God takes us through things to help us see ourselves completely. A strong identity in God has the understanding that "I am nothing without God". This understanding allows us to build an identity that will lift up our integrity over our own identity and image.

The identity of a human being is automatically an intangible layer of character as it is not something that can be touched. However, most people operate in their identity based on tangible things. Ignorantly, we associate the demeanor of our identity with the tangible elements that make up society's ideal image. We use education, titles, physical appearance, money, etcetera, to form an identity based on these ideals of the ideal image of mankind.

Such ideals as these are artificial characteristics that cause us to become artificial people. These characteristics are not original human traits. They cause us to behave as soulless beings if we dwell on these artificial attributes alone.

When we build an identity based upon what is tangible we allow an intangible part of our character to become susceptible to "tangibility." This means an intangible essence of who I am (identity in this case) becomes easily affected and influenced by tangible entities, commodities, or substances.

Our identity should be based upon entities, commodities, and substances that are intangible. These intangible entities, commodities, and substances should be of God's nature and what is acceptable in His sight. When we base and build our identity on what is intangible, our identity is not easily able to be defined or defiled by ourselves, other people, or Satan.

We hold the power of ultimately allowing ourselves to be defined or defiled. What we allow ourselves to be depends on our relationship with God. This determines how much we know the value that we are in God's eyes as His children.

Today, most people do not know their value in God, and because of this they are enslaved by the motives, methods, and mentalities of society. Being enslaved by society in this way clouds true identity and binds potential which withholds purpose. Therefore, we must step up to the plate of our integrity in God.

Integrity: The Essence that Really Matters

The deepest layer of people is integrity. Integrity is the most intangible part of a person. If image is the crust of a person, and identity is the mantle, integrity is the core. Integrity is the central and foundational distinctive part of human character by its difference in nature. It is the part of human character where our spiritual and natural natures collide.

Our integrity is the core layer of who we are and who we should be. Attributes that come with this layer of human character are all intangible factors. These intangible factors answer "why" we are the way we are. Integrity is the essence of a person that really matters as it can surpass time. It is the perspective of us that links us with purpose. Character has no guidance or guide lines without integrity which guides and frames us in our purpose.

Looking at American society today, one could say that integrity has become almost an extinct portion of character. However, integrity is what defines a decent identity and develops a distinctive image.

"If you don't stand for something, you'll fall for anything." This quote challenges us to live by standards that promote wholeness undefiled. What ever happened to standards in today's society?

The reality about the essence of each of us is that although we can hold ourselves to our own standard we can never be held accountable to who we are as a child of God unless we operate by God's standards. To reach our highest potential we have to step up to the plate of our integrity in God. We are so much more inside and we are beyond what we think we know about ourselves. How do we truly know who God is calling us to be, and for what purpose?

We make good strides toward living the intangible life by following visions that we believe God has given us, but first and foremost we ought to learn to work the vision God has already had in place- His Word. The Word of God is the vision of the standard God wants us to learn to live by. Learning to live by the Word of God is living by an intangible standard and that standard is based on love.

The problem that people have in reference to character is the lack of love. Not only do we lack in love, but we lack in love to the core. If we truly loved from the core of our being, I believe our love would remain pure. In fact, there is nothing more pure than to love from the core of who we are, more specifically the love that is of God.

When love is the root in the core of our integrity in God, our love comes from a pure and unconditional place. Love that comes from an intangible source fuels other intangible sources that fuel other intangible resources that we pull from. This process develops an intangible identity which will reflect an image formed from intangible substances. So understand human integrity of character, like the Earth's core, is what allows us to operate correctly. Without integrity of character we cannot operate properly, as God would like, and we would thereby, breakdown and deteriorate in our humanity.

The main idea is that integrity is the missing factor in today's society. I believe this is true in America as well as other nations around the world. The sad reality about the world's lack of integrity isn't just our lack of integrity from pure and secure resources. Integrity cannot be truly pure and secure when it is based and built upon tangible substances.

We live in a society that builds and bases integrity upon the tangible ideals of what defines decent character in man's eyes. Our degrees, our careers, the amount of money we make, even our intoxicated emotions are all tangible things that really cannot bear any weight when it comes to integrity. Our integrity starts from the spirit and requires no weight, neither is it a resource that can be weighed.

We can start from the bottom with no class and rise to the top and still have no class. By the same token, we can start from the top with no class and fall to the bottom and still have no class. True integrity is all about the spirit and has no respect of persons, just like the source it comes from- God. The source of true integrity comes from God.

God is love. Therefore, when our integrity comes from God it comes from a place of pure love. I often wonder if our view of love is equivalent to God's view of love. Can we even fathom God's definition of love, what it means to love, and even what love is and looks like through His eyes?

How can the created precisely grasp the Creator's ideal of the essence of what it is, who it is, and why it is? This philosophical question challenges us to step up to the plate of our integrity in God and be a better people beyond our own standards. By allowing our integrity in God to be the leading layer of our character we develop an identity in the likeness of Christ that depicts the right image of a child of God. This also distinguishes a character that God is pleased with, because it is a character that is led by God's Spirit.

~ *Chapter Two* ~

LOVE'S FACTUAL PHILOSOPHY

The Matter of the Heart

The most significant issue in the world today is a matter of the heart. People are walking around in society dead on the inside with hearts cold as ice because they have allowed unpleasant things to creep in their hearts and make a home. The state of humanity is dying from the inside out.

When I speak of the heart, I'm not referring to the natural organ, but I am referring to the essence of truth within us. The heart in the spiritual sense is the most deceitful part of us and this can affect our integrity. One of the reasons I believe it is deceitful is because the heart is cunning. However, if one can get to "the heart of the matter" one can find the motive, method, and mindset of the matter. "As a man thinks in his heart so is he."

The heart is the milestone of our intentions, our behaviors, and our thoughts. Everything that we want to know about an individual in truth is found in the heart. The heart can be a very crowded place because in it can reside both mess and majesty. "Where one's heart is can be found one's treasure." By the same token, where one's heart is can be found one's trash.

If mankind were machines the heart would be the motherboard. It is the main circuit of a human being that contains the path of all we are based upon what we have gathered in our experiences, observations, and awareness in life. Following the path of our hearts can be a dangerous journey if we are not aware and if we are not led by God first. In fact, it is better to follow God's heart and forsake the journey of your own heart where lies and deception may lurk.

The heart has a habit of playing against its keeper, just like the mind. Sometimes the heart and the mind work against each other, and other times they work with each other. However, very often they can work together against us, and when they work against each other, we, their host, are the ones who are being torn apart.

Have you ever been in the middle of conflict with your mind and your heart? When this happens we freeze. We don't freeze because we want to, we freeze because we're trapped and we can't figure out which is the safest direction to go. When this happens choose God's heart and mind. He is the Creator and Master of both, and they cannot work against Him.

The first step is giving God your heart and giving God your mind by committing them to Christ. This is how we get on one accord with God and in unity with one another. If we each individually give God our heart and mind we give God control of our intentions, our behaviors, and our thoughts, because we have placed them in His hands. In this manner we do what God orchestrates us to do, we know what God orchestrates us to know, and we can be who God orchestrates us to be.

Similarly, because we each have given our hearts and minds to God, all of our hearts and all of our minds can then be held in the same place (in God), and are orchestrated by the same hands. So now the Body of Christ can be in unity with one another because by this we are on one accord with God. It's not about getting on one accord with one another. This will never work with man. We have become too corrupt by nature.

It is rather about getting on one accord with God and this way everybody is moving in the same route. This is easier said than done, because many of us do not want to yield fully to the will of God. It is a process! However, our spiritual objective as God's children is to strive to be on one accord with God in order to be in unity with one another.

Our hearts and minds are precious to us just as they are precious to God, because in them both contain our will. This is what makes the heart and mind one in the same from the spiritual sense, although they are two different entities. However, I urge us to give the Creator what is rightfully His. God created our hearts and minds and gave them to us, but they really belong to Him and not us in essence of original ownership. How can we truly know our hearts and minds if we did not create them? In addition to this question, how can we master our hearts and minds if we are not their true master?

The answer is by giving God our soul because the soul contains the heart and the mind. So when we give God our soul we automatically relinquish our heart and mind to God. With this in mind, we should if we are saved. Does our soul truly belong with God? It all depends on a characteristic that our soul must carry. That characteristic is unconditional love!

Love, a Characteristic not an Attribute

Is love a part of me or is it apart of what people see in me? There is a difference! The difference is, love is either a part of me or it is apart from me. Love has to be found in me. It has to be in my blood. Love cannot be something attached or attributed in me. Love should be a part of who I am by nature.

Many of us have allowed the world to do spiritual plastic surgery on us. We have allowed the world to spiritually alter who we are. As a result, the procedure has caused love to be removed from us. In our corrupt desire for something else, we have lost love, which once was a part of who we were naturally. Sometimes we cannot receive something without losing something. Today's society is losing love- our natural love, and we are substituting it with contaminated love.

What makes love contaminated? Love is contaminated when it becomes a "tit for tat" thing. Today, people love based on expectation or necessity. It is almost a rare thing to see people love for the sake of love. This is evident in the world as well as the church. It is a corrupt behavior that believers of Christ and non-believers of Christ now both share.

In our ignorance we try to hide the fact that we lack in love. However, this is a characteristic that one cannot conceal. Either love is present within us or it is not. For the most part, love has become an absent characteristic within people in society and this is shamefully true for individuals who claim to be believers of Jesus Christ.

Pure love is a characteristic that identifies one as a child of God. Pure love is what people lack. It makes love sincere. If love is not sincere it is not pure. If love is not pure it is contaminated. When the love within us is contaminated we begin to deteriorate in our integrity in God as His children. Deteriorating in our integrity in God causes us to deface our identical image with Christ and makes it difficult for other people to be able to identify us as followers of Christ and thereby children of God.

I believe that man's perception of love since sin has entered the world, has plagued mankind over time, and has clouded our ability to see love as God sees love. Love is love and it is unconditional. So often, we make reference of how much we belong to God. We are God's children. We are God's chosen elect. We are made in God's image. But what is it that makes us children of God in essence? What makes us related to God?

If we are made in the image and likeness of God that means we look like God and that we carry characteristics that identify us as similar to God. Therefore, we should mirror God on the outside as well as mirror God on the inside. This is what makes character so important and why integrity is the essential part of our character. Our integrity again, is the core of who we are- the deepest part of who we are spiritually. Mirroring the image and likeness of God in our integrity reflects in our identity and shows in the image we display.

When we really understand that we are made in the image and likeness of God, we can comprehend that this means we inherit certain characteristics of God. This proves that we are children of God and that we are of God when we show features that resemble Him. If we mirror Christ, and that means we are identical in our characteristics with Christ and able to identify with him, we know we resemble God and that God will be pleased with us.

The Holy Spirit being present in us is how we know we identify with Christ. Being "doers" of what the Word of God says and not just "hearers" of the Word is how we show we are identical to Christ. Putting all this together, we learn what love is. We learn how to love. We also come to an understanding that pure love is the essential characteristic we have supernaturally inherited from God. Unfortunately, if we allow our hearts to become corrupt, we contaminate this love.

Being Proven in Love

If you are a believer, you may already have the understanding that "God is love" and that "perfect love cast out all fear." So when we understand who God is, we can understand what love is. Further, as God perfects us in time to the degree that He wants us to be, we no longer are fearful beings. Fear is what plagues our society and has held us back from loving the way we should.

There are plenty of reasons why fear has plagued people in today's society but the main reason we fear is because in our human nature we despise not being in control of our own lives. Yet in our ignorance, due to the deception of fear, we lose control by giving into fear, allowing fear to govern our lives. Love in its perfection in us allows us to be secure despite whatever goes on around us and allows us to show love for the sake of love. This is true and pure love.

We are perfected in God's love when we live a lifestyle that exhibits consistent obedience, reverence, and commitment to God based on the personal affirmation that God loves us. This takes getting personal with God which is a part of having a personal relationship with Him. It is because some of us are lacking a personal relationship with God that we are not made perfect in love.

The church has become systemized. A great portion of the church is operating as a worldwide international organization opposed to the guiding light of the world we should be. The church has made practice and has become perfect in operating the artificial motive, method, and mentality of "church." This has become so great a practice that the church has become an artificial body in the world. It has become another mechanical body among many systems of the world- a religion and not a body of believers living a certain lifestyle.

However, the church is supposed to be an authentic body. It is not an entity of religion. The church is a labeled entity that houses a group of people who live the Christian lifestyle. What has happened to the church is that it has become breached by the methods of the world and we have been infected with the world's corrupt motives and mentality that come from Satan. As a result, the church has lost the main characteristic that separates us from other entities in the world. This is all because we have disconnected from God, and in this same action we have disconnected from God's will and God's ways.

The church is a body of believers of Jesus Christ that through Christ we follow the method, motive, and mentality of God. God's method, motive, and mentality is centered and founded on love. When we disconnect from God we disconnect from the mentality of God and cannot operate to the effective standard He is pleased with. As a domino effect of disconnecting from God's mentality we also disconnect from His motive and method.

Why does this happen? This happens because we don't have a personal relationship with God. It makes it difficult for us to be intimate with God. To be intimate with God is to know God in a personal way and make a deep connection. Under these circumstances, the church cannot operate in love like God because it doesn't know God personally. Therefore, we cannot know the love He has for us individually. In order for the church to show God's love as a whole in the world, we have to personally know God's love for ourselves.

God knows us, but it is us who have forgotten Him. Yet we do recall Him! That is why when we behave in ways that is not like God (such as not loving like God loves) we feel funny, because deep on the inside we know God and we know by our integrity in God that something is wrong.

God is love and we are made in God's image and likeness from the inside out. Therefore, because we are made in the image and likeness of God, a part of who we are is also love by design and if we don't show it from the inside out (which is the genuine way of showing love) we are not being ourselves. That is what has made mankind in society today seem like more of artificial beings than the authentic beings

God has made us. We lack in love and that is not how we are made to act if we are God's children.

Satan's children have characteristics as their father. Love is not in them and cannot be expected from them. God's children inherit His characteristics inside of them. Therefore, love is in us and should be expected from us. We prosper and operate normal based upon what we are on the inside. As the children of God made in His image and likeness we are love. So why are we struggling to show the world who we are? Perhaps we don't know who we are because we don't know whose we are. We must let our light shine, exposing ourselves as the love we are.

Learning to Forgive

One of the most difficult things I had to learn to do and understand is how to forgive. The most difficult thing about forgiving others was getting comfortable with the fact that it takes time and it takes a willing heart. Not forgiving keeps us bound as we so often hear. The chains of not forgiving are like thin binds of iron wire that tangle the soul. These binds bind us tight and cut us as we try to get free which can be an excruciating process. However, it is an experience where once we become free the refreshing sense of liberty is like none other. It leaves us refined and sometimes close to immune to the individual we have been offended by. Imagine how much refinement and how much of a sense of immunity we would have if some of us could only forgive ourselves?

I personally struggled with forgiving others, because I didn't know how to forgive. Forgiving others was essential for me to do because I knew if I wouldn't forgive others who offended me, God would not be entitled to forgive me whenever I offend Him. I would often pray to God and ask him to teach me and show me how to forgive so that He could forgive me. I found that forgiveness is indeed a process that happens in time, but it really all starts with having the will in our hearts to forgive. We just have to wait out the process and understand our part in forgiving.

Let's face it! Some of us have some really tough and deep situations where we even wonder how we can forgive others who have offended us greatly. These situations could include heart break, molestation or rape, neglect from a parent, different forms of abuse, words, break of trust, even murder. However, God is bigger than all of these things and although some of these things we may not understand, God understands. Forgiveness takes obtaining a new mentality.

Everything is achieved through our mentality. Sometimes when the situations we face or have faced are too much for us to handle, we have to ask God to help us handle them or to handle it for us. If we do this with a sincere mind and a pure heart God will see us through. I know this from experience. I have been in situations that I was not sure how I was going to get over, but in time God freed me because I put God's mentality, motive, and method above my own in every situation.

After coming to understand forgiveness I arrived at the thought that forgiveness does two things. Forgiveness frees the offended from the offender, and teaches the offender how to handle the offended. Once I make up my mind in my heart that I need to forgive an individual so that I can move forward in my life, the process to freedom begins. It hurts at first, because we have to become immune to our offender, so God may cause us to run into this individual a few times during the healing process. How we react and behave in the presence of our offender lets us know just how ready to forgive we really are. Our hurt will tempt us to keep on hating. When this happens ignore the hurt.

Forgiveness also teaches our offender how to handle us- the offended. The way our offender learns how to handle us- the offended, is by how we handle them- our offender. "You teach people how to treat you." Our behavior, reaction, and composure, determines how our offender will react and behave toward us. If we show we are ready to move forward from the offence then our offender will pick this up spiritually, based on our composure.

Composure exists in our integrity. Remember integrity is reflected in identity which is revealed in image. By the same token, if we still show the same image of the person our offender has offended, we can't expect them to take pity on us and treat us differently than what they did, because they only know how to treat us as they know us. If we become a different person in our core, then they have no choice but to handle us differently, because they are dealing with a different person in essence. See how powerful our spiritual man is?

There are some people who will never know how to handle us or care for handling us the right way. These folk we have to remain free from and let them go, because if we hold on to them, we run the risk of becoming bound again in an even tighter bind than before. We also run the risk of becoming the offender, and thereby, we become no better than they are.

It is not about being better than anyone. However, as children of God and advocates for Christ we have to carry ourselves differently and hold ourselves to a higher standard. We must always "press toward the mark of the high calling of Jesus Christ." In this way God is pleased with us and will even handle our problem even better than we could. There is nothing more satisfying and nothing more liberating than to not care about what others who mean us no good think about us.

The major problem we make that puts us in the same boat with our offender, is our corrupt ways we "adjust" in forgiving others. Sometimes we purposely adjust the wrong way and label it the right way of forgiving because this way makes us feel better. However, right is right and wrong is wrong. There are no alternatives concerning the right way to forgive.

Some of us in the church, from leaders to lay members, are adjusting our need to forgive. We carry the mindset such as, for example, forgiving our offender, but having nothing to do with them. This is because we're actually still angry and have not fully forgiven them yet. In our corrupt ways we call this "adjusting" and claim it is to protect ourselves. But is this real freedom?

I understand that for some people in our lives who've offended us, we need to make "adjustments," and in this case, some folk may have to be adjusted out of our lives. However, when it comes to family or relationships where inevitable bonds exist, what we require is on a whole different level. On this level not only do we require the need to forgive, we require the need for deliverance. The people of God have a bad habit of accepting delivery but not getting delivered. In other words, we accept instruction but don't follow up with what was instructed especially when it comes to checking our own selves despite hurt or adversity.

There are cases where someone who offended us actually makes the first step to apologize, and we never accept the apology. Yet we wonder why we're still bound. We remain bound because we often make the decision to move on and not move forward. Moving on and moving forward are two different things. Moving forward is making progression without baggage. Moving on is making progress with baggage.

We walk around angry, tired, depressed, and fearful because we still carry the weight of things in the past. The shameful part is that we don't have to, and we shouldn't as children of God. God is a parent and He will not tolerate His children being at odds with one another. "A house divided against its self shall not stand." Are we the reason why the church stumbles? Are we the reason why the church is falling?

We must get our house in order and by house I mean our hearts. We struggle to forgive like Christ because we are not perfect in the love of God opposed to how Christ was. So many of God's children claim they want their crown but they don't want to show mercy by will of sacrificing their own ungodly pride so that God may be glorified. If we want our crown, we have to learn to sacrifice by showing mercy instead of sacrificing everything else.

"Obedience is better than sacrifice." So we have to remember that God wants us to show mercy not offer sacrifices that are actually corrupt lies because we want to do the "Christian" thing without dealing with the truth of our own ungodly selves.

~ Chapter Three ~

EVALUATING SELF VALUE

Interpreting Our Value

In addition to love, we have to love ourselves. We should love ourselves based on the value of God's love for us. It is also important to "love our neighbor as ourselves," as Christ commanded us. But what happens when the love we have for ourselves is very low or not present at all? How many of us actually love ourselves enough to show this toward others properly? We have to remember to "acknowledge God in all our ways; trusting in Him, and not leaning to our own understanding."

Some of us do not value ourselves in high esteem. We don't view ourselves as God views us, and as a result, we don't value ourselves as God values us. People who do value themselves in an ungodly prideful way tend to view themselves from a perspective too low or too high. This is due to ignorance of value based on one's own view. Ignorance of value increases the chance of violating self or allowing one self to be violated.

There is no explanation for this other than the fact that it is difficult for the created to see its true value from the Creator's point of view. Further, when we (the created) don't spend time daily getting to know God (the Creator) we remain ignorant of how much God really values us. Lacking personal relationship with God causes us to misinterpret our value due to lack of faith. When we lack in faith we lack in our ability to become knowledgeable of God's value of us.

God truly cares for us and everything that affects us. If we continue to ignore becoming personal with God by not sharing our cares with Him, we'll remain ignorant of how much God really cares. How will we know God cares for us if we neglect to trust Him with our cares?

God is caring enough of us to prove to us that He values us when we give Him the opportunity. All we have to do is trust Him. Trusting God is a matter of mind over matter, if we give God our mind He'll handle our matter.

People misinterpret their value when they leave their value in the hands of other people. Some people may be able to see our value and may be able to handle us properly, but we should never place our value in a person's hands or anything that is tangible. Our value isn't tangible, so we can't hope to become secure in our value based upon anything tangible. Our value is intangible, and anything intangible is best left in the hands of God. God is sovereign and is not subject to anything tangible or intangible.

The Measure of Our Value

The mistake we often make is putting our value on a scale system. The moment we equate our value on any scale system is the moment we label what we're worth. As a result, we put ourselves up for sale. Again, people tend to label their value too low or too high. Despite either way, labeling our value with what we think we're worth is evidence of insecurity.

Do we really know how much we're worth in God's eyes? In God's eyes we are priceless because we are His children. We are the workmanship of God. He sees us as priceless art. He is the Master artist who cherishes His work.

God has meaning and purpose for everything He makes and because of this we are valuable.

We have to be careful with the mentality that causes us to put worth on ourselves. Who are we to say how much we're worth? We didn't create ourselves so we don't have a right to label ourselves. In fact, when we put a "price tag" on ourselves we are defacing God's property.

Our lives are not our own. We all belong to God. We're out of place when we put ourselves up for sale in any form or fashion. Who are we to sell someone else's property? We take ownership of God's property when we claim ownership of ourselves.

God is an artist and like, Erykah Badu says, "God is sensitive about His stuff." When we label or claim God's stuff as our own in action or attitude, He does feel some type of way about it. It is an insult to God.

We should have enough reverence to respect ourselves as the property of God. We respect ourselves by acknowledging that we are God's. This respect comes from our awareness of the love of God which is found in Jesus Christ. When we become "saved" we re-dedicate ourselves to

God's standard and not our own. God's standard is Christ, and Christ is His Word (the Bible).

Accepting Jesus Christ as our personal Lord and Savior is the first step of dedicating ourselves to live by God's standard. God's standard challenges and causes us to step up to the plate of our integrity in Him. By accepting the challenge we live a life of refined and not defined value. This raises the bar of our value as we then live a lifestyle based upon God's perspective.

Misplacing the Wealth we are

Some of us question our value despite the fact that we sense greatness inside us. The fact that we are insecure or ignorant in this sense of greatness within us is a challenge to acknowledge who we really are in God. Some folk look to people to verify what lies inside of them and thereby remain insecure. Never place the security of yourself in the tangible hands of others.

Putting our security in the hands of people makes us susceptible to their opinion. The opinions of people often change, so when our security is placed in the hands of people, our security is also susceptible to that change. How can we be secure in constant shifting?

When security constantly shifts it makes it difficult to have a secure foundation to be grounded in. This is similar to a foster child who moves from home to home based on a tangible system. A foster child never gets permanently settled in a family because of the constant moving whenever the system says it's time to move. One cannot allow their value to become susceptible to a tangible system. One never becomes thoroughly grounded in their value when it is always shifting. Someone in this position will continue to be insecure in who they are because they were never grounded.

We cannot become truly confident in how God desires to work in us until we become confident in knowing that God is the direct source working in us with or without people. We show this confidence when we understand that we don't need people to validate who we are or what we are capable of. Whenever we seek the validation of our value from people and not God we make idols out of those people.

We are not ready to be used by God if He is in second place. God must always be first. When God is first, we are acknowledging that He is solely in control and we are whole by this knowing. This completes us! It allows us to be in need of nothing, especially the validation of people.

One of the most challenging things we face in life is being confident in God's sole approval alone despite the opinions of others. God's decisions are absolute. So in spite of people saying we are not something, we can be assured that if God says we are something, we are who God says we are. We must be confident in God's value of us. We are able to be confident of our value in God by His approval which comes by the assurance of His Word as we study the Bible that contains it.

~ Chapter Four ~

IT'S ALL ABOUT THE SPIRIT

Intimate Refinement

I believe that we've all experienced a period in our existence before birth where we had an intimate relationship with God. "I knew you before I formed you in your mother's womb. Before you were born I set you apart and appointed you a prophet to the nations." (Jeremiah 1:5). I like to imagine that the life we live on Earth is a journey back to our initial place of intimacy with God. This ideal reminds us that though life may seem very physical, it is a spiritual journey to redemption.

We are redeemed through Christ; living a refined life in him toward the restoration of our initial intimate place with God. This place with God is the source of our essential creation. What a thought, that each of us in eternity has had a relationship with God. We just don't remember!

The life we live as flesh in blood is nothing compared to eternal life where only our spiritual nature can dwell. "Flesh and blood cannot enter the Kingdom of God," yet ignorantly, people focus more on a temporal life than the eternal life that awaits them. The choice of which life we view more important makes a difference in the character and lifestyle we choose to live after.

Our lives are not measured in years, but they are rather measured in how we live our lives and the mark we leave in this world. We leave our mark in this world by living a legacy life. A legacy life is a lifestyle of destiny; a divinely purposed life. God gives us all that we need to live up to who He has destined us to be.

When I think about the calling of God on my life, I think about how amazing it is that God's voice is ultimately familiar to me. That's what I view intimate refinement to be all about: Answering God's call by faith and being refined in the destiny He places on our lives; and in addition, acknowledging God from a sense of knowing Him intimately opposed to intellectually.

The amazing thing about the call of God is that it's an experience of recollection. We recall what we were called to do as we know the voice giving us the task to perform it. Today, God is calling His children and many are recollecting His voice.

However, it seems as though we are responding to God's call as an act of obligation and not opportunity. The difference is revealed in our attitude in our performance of the call. The call of God should be treated as a privileged opportunity and an invitation to divine ordained destiny. When destiny is upon us, we can't afford to miss it. Destiny is bound to happen. It is our purpose.

The Right Spirit

Spirituality in modern society has become tainted. While it is not ignored it has become under-valued when we consider how serious people take it. The only time we seem to include spirituality is when dealing with abnormal folk in society.

In addition, spirituality seems to be considered as just another way to categorize people in society for the benefit of satisfying comfort opposed to truth. People today of various ages, ethnicities, and general background deem themselves as "spiritual". In Philadelphia alone, if we took a tour of the hood we would notice a large amount of people who appear to practice Islam. However, many who appear or claim to practice Islam when you turn a blind eye seem to not practice it as much as they say. I may not practice Islam, but I know enough to understand it is a faith that emphasizes integrity and honorable discipline.

It amazes me how often I see people claiming to be "Muslim" displaying themselves opposite of this character of integrity and honor. The same can definitely be said for faithful "Christians" who "shout" every Sunday and display ungodly character Monday through Saturday. But the bottom line seems to be that spirituality in society has become corrupt across the board.

It has become a subject of socialization and not heart felt truth. This is because society is not chasing after the right Spirit. How many of us before choosing to practice a religion, have actually considered the sole purpose of what we're practicing? Many folk don't. No, people nowadays choose to believe in what is comfortable or won't convict them.

Now in some cases this is understandable. If one grows up in a family that practices Christianity, more than likely that individual will continue to do so. However, what I noticed today is that there are many individuals, primarily youth, who do grow up in families where the majority of them are Christian but the majority of the youth's social circle are Muslim. As they socialize with their Muslim friends they seem to experience more comfort being themselves. In addition, they become more familiar with Islam in the process. Before we know it that individual conforms in thought from being around Islam consistently, and the next thing we see, they're "garbed up".

I have asked individuals in this same situation, "what caused them to make the change?" All their answers seemed to be, "I just felt Christianity wasn't for me and I felt this was a better decision to make." Not once did I get a real answer that would describe how the decision was made based on sole examination. Each had given answers based on social comfort. Further, they all seemed insecure and defensive about their reasoning for making their decision.

Their answers were all similar in that they struggled to live out the Christian walk. More importantly, they were either not firm in their personal knowledge of Christ, or they deferred to various carnal reasons.

Carnality or the opinions of others should never be a factor in spiritual choices. The decision one makes as it relates to the soul should be made between one's self and God.

The problem with spirituality in society today is that it has been tainted so much by the blending of other spiritual factors. In addition, spirituality in the world has done a job twisting the total identity of Jesus Christ and distorting the doctrine of the trinity. Accepting Jesus Christ in his totality changes things and brings truth even when it hurts. Jesus provides us with the "Holy Spirit who leads us into all truth".

The Holy Spirit is so powerful that the effect he makes in the supernatural pours out onto the natural. It's a feeling that cannot be controlled because it cannot be described and it cannot be described because people can't understand it in their mere natural reasoning.

People can't understand it because they don't know it. They don't know it because they don't know God. Those who know God belong to Him and recognize His voice; they are His children. When God calls, those who answer His call, belong to God because they recall His voice: "My sheep listen to my voice; I know them, and they follow me (John 10:27 NLT)."

As children of God we are predestined to answer God's call. Since we are predestined to answer God's call, we are refined as His chosen elect. As His elect "we are called, we are justified, and we are glorified."

In this, we are called back into a personal relationship with God. As children of God, we are justified by the suffering, death, and resurrection of Jesus Christ. As children of God, we are glorified because of the victory of Christ over sin, death, and Hell.

However, "many are called but few are chosen". This is why many who hear the voice of God reject the call. They refuse in their hearts to know Him. These people will never know God because they reject His Son and so they don't receive the Holy Spirit that can lead them in seeing the truth of who God is.

However, the Holy Spirit rejected or not, cannot be ignored in peace. For this reason, many turn away or reject anyone who the Holy Spirit lives in. The Holy Spirit is the right Spirit. The Holy Spirit is the light of truth that believers carry in a society blinded in the darkness of lies.

Fearfully and Wonderfully Made

Everything God has made was made in decency and in order. As I heard someone mention in a video I was watching, "everything God has created works like a clock". God has caused everything to function together in unity and for a purpose; a purpose that is selfless, righteous, and prosperous.

God has made every human being in three total portions. We are made with a body, a mind, and a spirit. Each portion of who we are share and take part in all the experiences of our reality. Our body, mind, and spirit, also have similar senses. The only difference is that our body has tangible senses. Our mind has intangible and tangible senses. Our spirit has intangible senses. Our mind bridges the gap between the senses of our body and spirit. Our body and spirit have opposing senses, but our spiritual senses are more powerful and affective.

Although our body, mind, and spirit, are different portions of our being, they are similar in how they operate. All three are living portions that require nourishment, nurturing, grooming, and discipline. They only experience and receive these things at different levels and dimensions. If we want to feed our body for nourishment, we eat food. If we want to feed our mind for nourishment, we take in knowledge. If we want to feed our spirit for nourishment, we consume spiritual things like reading the Word.

God has made every portion of our being different but they operate very similarly. The only portions that conflict because of their opposing natures, one being tangible, the other being intangible, are our body and spirit.

The mind, being found effective both tangibly and intangibly, is the middle portion of our being. Whichever portion between our body and spirit that we nourish, nurture, groom, and discipline more, is how the mind will operate. It's almost as if our mind sides with whichever portion is stronger. Our spirit and body fight for the allegiance of the mind to claim dominance over us.

Since the fall of mankind we have been separated from God because of sin that corrupted us. I believe the cleverness of Satan is found in that he was able to deceive us by causing us to see ourselves as less than what we actually were. What Satan did was take his corrupt traits of character as a former servant and creation of God and introduce us to the same corruption. He deceived us by planting the same seed of foolish curiosity he had in himself.

There are three attributes of character that are referred in the Word of God as wicked and ungodly. Those attributes are selfishness, pride, and jealousy. These three attributes do not contribute to the progress of mankind in unity, nor are they in accord with God's pleasure. They contradict the progress of mankind in unity and in accord with God's pleasure.

The attributes that contribute to the progress of mankind in unity in accord with God's pleasure I have found to be stewardship, grace, and mercy. I believe these three attributes are what people commonly lack worldwide. When we fail to show one another stewardship, grace, and mercy, which are attributes of love, God is not pleased with us. God is love and despite our corrupt state, He shows these attributes to us through the grace of Jesus Christ.

We continue to fail in showing these attributes and we further corrupt them by compromising and contradicting them. What is stewardship? It's being a caretaker for God by nurturing what belongs to Him. What is grace? It is unmerited favor. What is mercy? Mercy is showing compassion, showing love, and more importantly, giving love through patience and close consideration.

By the world's standard these attributes of character are deemed weak because in mans' eyes they are attributes of a servant and not of royalty, and certainly not of a god. The dark reality is that we want to be God by exact identity.

By God's standards these attributes are exactly what it takes and what it means to be great. They are what it takes to be godly, and they are characteristics of what it means to be royalty. To grasp understanding of the importance of assimilating these godly and righteous attributes is to be transformed into a new creature by conforming to Jesus Christ. The result of this makes one peculiar and sanctified on Earth despite the constraints that the world imposes.

Truth is, today's society does not understand the nature of God's pleasure. If society did understand the nature of God's pleasure we would value God more and value each other better. We are God's pleasure when we become who He has designed us to be. Human nature is artificial when it is centered on self which is birthed from fear.

Fear is the real reason why people under value God and mishandle one another. God created mankind in love.

Love is our nature, not fear. Love is not selfish, prideful, or jealous- these are the attributes of fear not love. We're too afraid to live for one another, so we're selfish. We're too afraid to dare to be different by showing grace, so we bask in our pride. We're too afraid to humble ourselves and admit someone is doing better, so we are consumed in jealousy.

Love is the answer to who we really are, who we are meant to be. We are to be love like God, our Creator. The greatest life we can live in freedom is a life as a slave of God. I believe this is God's definition of a ruler and someone great. "The greatest among you must be a servant. But those who exalt themselves will be humbled, and those who humble themselves will be exalted (Matthew 23:11-12)." Love is what God uses to compel us in faith "to will and to do His good pleasure."

~ Chapter Five ~

THY KINGDOM COME, THY WILL BE DONE!

Case Managers by Nature

We are all case managers by nature. Our divine job is to operate in the spirit of ministry and stewardship. Performing well in this job is knowing that stewardship and ministry go hand and hand. One cannot minister without operating in the spirit of stewardship. One cannot show stewardship without operating in the spirit of ministry.

As God's children, "we are ministers and stewards on account of the mysteries of God." Everything has an order. As we are God's offspring and are made in His image and likeness, this challenges us to operate as He operates. When it comes to developing into who God has created us to be we must grasp that the natural occupation of people who reverence God is ministry and stewardship.

Humanity's natural design was never to be about glorifying self and being centered in one's self, but rather the contrary. Human beings are originally and naturally designed to be stewards- servants by God's authority. Serving by God's authority is ministry.

By spiritual decree, we are God's stewards over the Earth which is a service more than a privilege. By spiritual duty, we are also ministers over the Earth which is the action in our service of stewardship that we have inherited as God's children. Our duty is to minister to the needs of the Earth in truth and love. Mankind has lost sight of what stewardship and ministry actually is by God's standards due to sin nature entering the world (Genesis 3).

As a result, we became corrupt which has perverted generations of mankind further, in a "domino effect" all the way up to today. This domino effect corrupts the state of who we were by original design, which effects our character and in this our role as God's stewards of the Earth.

Where we were once most like God, we were deceived and made corrupt in nature. Our character and everything associated with our character was altered, including our occupation as stewards and ministers. In regard to our character, I have found Adam and Eve's disobedience to God to be an offense of commission regarding their integrity in God, opposed to an offense of omission regarding their identity in God. I believe that Adam and Eve's offense of commission was a result of insecurity and ignorance of their identity in God. If Adam and Eve were secure in knowing who they were based upon who they belonged to, they may have remained secure in the state of who they were.

This is just a thought, but the ideal of this thought has affected mankind today. Sadly, we still don't know who we are because we are too naive to accept the truth that we are God's property.

People have always had a nasty habit of wanting to be God's equal and not God's people. Yet God still remains "merciful to the unthankful and the wicked" beings we remain to be toward Him. Through Jesus Christ, by God's grace, we are adopted as His children despite the fact that we always were His children, and chose to stray away willingly like the Prodigal son (Luke chapter 15). However, "We are still God's offspring" by His initial design of us.

Today, people continue to try to disprove God's relevance and existence. These people are bitter children who don't want to accept a Father they cannot fully understand. People seek out and depend on science and deem it wise; not accepting that either way we, the created, will always be under a higher authority, rather that authority be God to some or science to others.

People favor science because they can prove it. They can understand it because it is able to be calculated and figured out. Science is logic developed through logic, even if the logic comes by accident. In essence, science is falsifiable- "able to be proven or declared false". So if we are able to prove or declare something false, then potentially, we could have the ability to conquer and control it.

This would give us the potential to overrule what we are ruled by. My point being, if we can understand something to the point that we can control or conquer it, we can potentially become its equal and potentially learn to overrule it; in this case, overrule God. I believe that some people would like to rule over God just as Satan wanted to rule over Him. This shows us how much society is under satanic influence.

Developing Children in God

When it comes to personal development it is essential to start from the inside out. As a youth mentor, I have been asked by programs to speak to a number of youth about the topic of "professional development" opposed to personal development. However, considering the mindsets of youth I mentor, I have found giving tips about professional development to be void and ineffective.

Today's youth and troubled people don't need to be taught about professional development. What these people need is to be re-educated, enriched, empowered, and encouraged on the topic of personal development. To simplify, let's focus primarily on "at-risk" youth.

I have found that giving at-risk youth professional development tools is not very effective in actually sparking an internal positive change. I believe at-risk youth and young people today in general need tools to become professionals at being people of integrity. Giving our young people tools and training in professional development may do a justice when we consider the impact that the people presenting the tools may have on them, like the example they display themselves.

However, what happens when that person is gone and the time comes where the youth has to face their reality in the streets that they have to return to?

Returning to the same demonic influences and corrupt streets that they want to escape from is the "going in circles" reality for many youth. This is the same across the board, and includes even the youth in the hood who may do well and go to college, like myself. Despite what statistics may show, today's at-risk youth usually remain in the same streets they come from and many youth from the hood who do well and go off to college don't come back to their old neighborhoods.

This causes a cycle of ignorance that continues to plague and haunt each latter generation of at-risk youth such as peers, siblings, and relatives. Why? Because this leaves no relatable role model around to show our young people in the hood anything different. Why? Because the hood youth who graduate from college often don't return directly to the streets or they are conformed to a person the streets cannot recognize. A good number of them go away to different locations with friends they've made in college. So all the at-risk youth have left as relatable examples are people who are also at-risk who never left the hood.

Being a member of the hood myself, I see that there is a distinct image that our youth follow after. This image is really a spiritual influence to keep bound those God is calling to be most effective in the world. The ideal image of the hood has a distinct appearance, language, mindset, attitude, religious belief, and life goal. None of these distinctions seem centered around Christ. The "red flag" that goes up in my spirit based on what I see in Philadelphia alone, is the bondage of generational curses set up specifically by Satan to keep the hood in his possession.

We are no longer bound to generational curses, as Jesus Christ came to break generational curses. Jesus himself came from the hood too. He did great things beyond what was expected of him despite the negative labels placed on him because of where he came from. "Can any good thing come out of Nazareth? (John 1:46)" Satan knows that if God can bring forth greatness out of Nazareth, that God can still bring forth greatness out of any hood today. Satan will try to do anything to keep people who are significant and good for God's purpose from coming out of places like the hood, because these individuals have the potential to reach many lives. These individuals have the potential to save many souls similar to themselves.

Satan fears what may happen to the world he has ensnared if anything from places so constrained by fear, anger, foolishness, oppression, and despair, can rise to compel the world. Therefore, the Satanic influenced society desires the hood to be what it is statistically, in order to keep God's significant chosen ones trapped. But I believe God has a plan even bigger than this that is going to shock Satan in his plan. I believe God is going to set his chosen ones free, who are in bondage in the hood. He will do it by filling the enemy's "concentration camps"- the hood, with His Word.

The Word of God is the strongest and most relevant factor that our youth and people in general need considering personal development. The Word develops the spirit which in turn develops the person. It gives the person life. Our youth need personal development over professional development because before one can master the tools for being a professional on the job, one has to master the tools of being a person. We train our young people to know what's necessary to land a job but we don't give them the tools for maintaining a job.

What our youth need to be taught today more than ever is how to obtain and hold on to their integrity in God. One can go to even higher heights without the necessary credentials when one has integrity. Integrity is a rare trait among people, especially our youth today. When people see integrity in an individual youth, that youth stands out. In fact, people with God given sense will open up windows of opportunity because of the integrity that is shown.

We don't teach our youth the simplest factor when it comes to progressing from obtaining favor with people. That simple factor is that people will do things for you just off the strength that they like you. Somewhere in modern society we have developed an unspoken crazy ideal that people will hire us based on our credentials alone. No, credentials show qualification but credentials do not prove our quality.

Qualification is in actuality an element of quantity that adds to the appearance of quality. However, although qualification adds to quality it is still a quantitative factor because it is an element that presents tangible data as leverage. So qualification is just another part of tangible image as opposed to quality that is an element of intangible integrity.

Youth who live in urban communities, where opportunities are low and tragedies are high, need to be shown the quality that exist inside of them. Quality is more easily recognized when building up the person internally opposed to externally. There is no greater quality one can have greater than the Holy Spirit whom we only receive through Jesus Christ.

Christ is the neglected and only factor that produces true change. Teaching personal development as developed out of the Word of God, and sticking to what the Bible says about how a person should be and grow, is the best way to plant seeds of progress, success, and positive change in our youth.

To do this is very daring, but it is effective and people understand. We must keep in mind that the language we speak when sharing the Word of God as subject matters concerning personal development is best effective when acknowledging the nature of the language our audience speaks. Furthermore, we cannot be ignorant of the mindset that our audience has, rather the audience consist of youth, adults, or senior citizens. Asking the Holy Spirit on what to say and letting Him guide us on the manner of what we say and how we say it, is a must when taking this approach.

The Most Important Thing in Life

My mom always taught my sister and me that "the most important thing in life is a personal relationship with God." She said personal relationship with God should always come first before money, health, education, titles, status, favor, etc. In recent years, I found this to be absolutely true. A personal relationship with God gives one access to all things.

People in the world, especially Christians, claim to have a personal relationship with God but their concerns and attitudes toward their desires say otherwise. Personal relationship with God is not a complicated thing it is simply a personal relationship with God. People should consider if they really know God. Better yet, perhaps we should ask ourselves, as my uncle Charles would ask people, "Have we found Him?" God is not hard to find. In order to find God, we need only to read the Word to learn more about Him and examine ourselves based upon His standards.

Obtaining a personal relationship with God is something people make complicated? However, the answer is so simple many people miss it. The key thing is having a willing heart to follow Christ. It takes a God given desire to remain obedient and trust that God knows best. First, we need the Word of God. Secondly, we need a God given desire to obey God. But the most important thing is God's Word. Having a Bible means nothing if we don't make use of it. Bibles are for studying for God's approval not reading for theory and ego tripping.

Many know a lot of scriptures in the Bible and have its content down pact. However, they struggle to live by the Word themselves because they have not allowed it to transform their minds. This happens when people fill their minds with the Word but neglect to soak it into their hearts.

People enjoy the wisdom of God's Word. It makes them look good and seem wise- ego tripping. By the same token, people have fun going to church now. There's dancing, shouting, people get to show off their singing skills, and the latest fashion. However, the reality is, the people of this nature know church but they don't know the Word.

There is a way one lives and behaves when they actually have a personal relationship with God. When in a relationship one spends time with another, talking with them, doing things to please them, and in time, one picks up the other's traits. One also makes mistakes in relationships, but when this happens, one makes effort to right the wrong.

The same goes with being in a relationship with God. The problem is people don't personalize themselves with the person of God. Instead, people tend to overthink who God is. God is God, but because of our corrupt human nature we hate to submit to anything higher than our actual being. We fail and refuse to relate to God's person.

For this reason people refrain to pray to God, until we feel like we absolutely need God. Praying is how we commune with God verbally. If we refrain from communing with God, we prevent ourselves from having a relationship with Him. What healthy relationship do we know last without communication? Our communication to God shows our interest in Him. Our interest in God is a reflection of our love for Him.

When we don't talk to God, it's as if we don't love God and aren't that much into Him. Therefore, why should God be into us? Interestingly enough, I see how much society has grown comfortable ignoring God. We have come to this state in society because of the lack of personal relationships that exist among people and God individually.

Some of us only focus on the life we have on Earth, ignoring the life that will remain after we die. We act as though the life we live on Earth is our one and only stop. However, we are all spiritual beings, and the bodies we have are only shells that cover the essence of what we actually are. There will never be a moment in time or eternity that the spiritual part of our being will not exist (see 2 Corinthians 5:8).

Imagine yourself not existing. Even thinking about it is straining on the mind and heavy on the heart. It's almost farfetched and it brings much fear naturally because it's hard to see a world without ourselves. How could we? We wouldn't even exist to know what that would look like.

Society fails to have a personal relationship with God because we are so busy fearing God because we don't understand everything about Him. I believe that this is a fact that has caused us to reject God. As a result, people settle in their logic and reason and reject faith in God.

If one does not try to trust, one will never grasp having faith. Without faith in God we fail to love Him. God desires mankind to want Him sincerely. We should know this despite how cold hearted and tough we have become. People have an intangible itch for being wanted by those we love.

I see the world rejecting love for one another which is a result of lack of faith in God. Faith in God is the essential factor we need to have a personal relationship with God. "Without faith it is impossible to please God." Without faith there is no intimacy with God.

Once people learn to love God and gain a relationship with Him, humanity will be able to relate back to one another properly in love. True unity will not occur in society until we get on one accord with God. Man fails because instead of putting our faith in God's hands we place our faith in each other or ourselves. We put our faith in God's hands by building a foundation on Christ by studying the Word intimately.

Knowing the Word intimately requires us to listen and understand the Word. Listening and understanding are the pillars of proper and effective communication with God. We listen to understand and by this we gain understanding of the importance of listening. The result of the two is hearing what the Holy Spirit is saying to us. "He that has an ear let him hear." Are we listening to the voice of God found in His Word? God has done more than tell us what He wants. God has shown us!

Knowing who we are in Christ

In addition to having a personal relationship with God, we desire to know who we are too. Many people are not secure in knowing who they are. They don't know who they are because they don't see their purpose. They don't see their purpose because they don't know who to live for.

As children of God it is essential for us to know who we are in Christ. When we don't know who we are spiritually we are easily made into someone we are not destined to be through tangible influences. These factors can be the opinions of others, materialistic things, or the deceptive desires of our own hearts.

People desire to have balance in their lives because they want security. Balance doesn't come into our lives until we become secure in Christ. As my mom often says, "Jesus is the equalizer." Christ is the one who causes us to find out who we are after we find out who He is.

For those of us who don't know who we are in Christ in detail, the one thing we are for sure is successful. We are successful because we are called, justified, and glorified by the blood of Jesus Christ. Now we can stop chasing success as the world sees it and let it take form in our lives as we remain in Christ. We cannot see the formation of our true identity as successful beings until we identify with who Jesus is, mirroring the success that exist in us through Christ. We are led into success through the guidance of the Holy Spirit. "Not by power, not by might, but by God's Spirit."

People, places, and things will always try to define us. It's up to us to seek God as followers of Christ by being "doers" of the Word, living how the Bible tells us to live to avoid being a person of definition. If Satan can define us, he will have no problem identifying us, labeling us as his own children.

We must avoid the set up in a society that shows us that we need certain people, places, and things in order to be somebody. Everybody is somebody because God didn't make junk when He made us. We are each unique to God because He took His time to be intimate and make us how He wanted to make us. With God there is no need to be defined because He already defined us when He created us.

We are all precious in God's sight- like precious jars of art in His "pottery". God has given us the choice of being jars of trash or jars of treasure. Everyone has a role to play for

God's purposes. We make the choice of which jar we will be. God is merciful enough to allow us to choose what role we play according to His grace given to us through Jesus Christ. We have the power to instill our mark in the world as either vessels of honor or vessels of dishonor. So which vessel are you?

A major part of knowing who we are in Christ is being confident about who we are, and being refined in this. It is also about leaving a legacy life in the world by living after the legacy of Jesus Christ. In understanding this and living it out, we find that Christ's legacy fits into our lives like a puzzle. "All things work together for the good of those who love God." Knowing who we are in Christ is all about conforming to Him by His Word.

Knowing who we are in Christ is a refining and not a defining experience. With each refining experience we gain in Christ, one will develop some defining moments. In these moments we come to an intimate recognition in knowing in ourselves who we are in Jesus. This recognition is a knowledge we obtain in each moment of our lives in time, pressing toward life eternal in God. Sadly, people in Hell are folk who never discovered who they really are because they never knew the source of their being – Jesus Christ.

Our Best Friend

I mentioned earlier, that people are case managers by nature. In modern day society, the field of social service is engulfing the United States. I know this to be an unspoken fact in Philadelphia. Being a case manager myself, I noticed in my home town of Philadelphia, that almost everyone seemed to have a case manager. Now this may not mean anything to you, but to me, this was indeed an eye opener of how much people have become comfortable with depending on one another opposed to depending on God.

Have we become weak as a society? Have we forgotten God to the point that we can no longer stand confidently on His word and in our faith in Him? Perhaps we have chosen to ignore God purposely because we think we want to be in total control of our own lives. We choose to depend on man whom we understand opposed to God whom we don't understand. We choose not to depend on God because we won't take time to come to know Him. Depending on God requires us to include God in our lives. The more we learn how much we actually depend on God, the more we will include Him in every portion of life.

As we include God in every portion of our lives, we develop a stronger bond in our personal relationship with God. The bond we develop with God deepens our companionship with Him. The Holy Spirit is our greatest companion and he is "a friend that sticks closer than any brother". The Holy Spirit is capable of being all we need him to be on any level. He is a guide, a teacher, and an advocate. Anything we need him to be that is within the will of God, the Holy Spirit is that!

Peoples' lack of trust in God is what keeps the Holy Spirit from being all they need Him to be because they haven't accepted Christ to receive Him. The only way we can receive the Holy Spirit is to receive Him as a gift which we receive after accepting Jesus Christ as our personal Lord and Savior. Then, we receive the Holy Spirit and get access to His instruction that informs us of what to do according to the will of God. I believe the Holy Spirit's instruction is unique to all of us as individuals. However, I also believe that the Holy Spirit speaks to all of us in the same intimate place, which is in our hearts and minds.

When we receive the Holy Spirit, the will of our thoughts becomes connected to the will of God's thoughts. By the Holy Spirit and God's Word, we have access to God's will as it relates to His purpose for us and the world. Unfortunately, some people don't have access to the insight of the Holy Spirit because they reject the full truth of Jesus Christ. This is why I think people in the world today behave so carelessly, as if they are empty inside.

The will and conscience of a human being without the instruction of the Holy Spirit is very dangerous, corruptible, and unstable. Without the acknowledgment and guidance of the Holy Spirit people are easily subject to demonic forces. Anyone subject to demonic forces is already an open target for Satan to possess.

"It's all about the spirit," and for human beings, our minds are pawns to either God or Satan. As long as our souls are "free agents" in their allegiance, our souls are free to be used and moved by either God or Satan as well. Freewill isn't so fun in the midst of the spiritual activity that is roaming freely in the world today.

Freewill takes discipline. This discipline must come with the conviction of the Holy Spirit. We each make the conscience choice freely of how we will serve God's will. Will we fulfill God's will by serving Him in Christ through the empowering of the Holy Spirit? Or will we fulfill God's will dishonorably by serving Him under the ignorant influence of Satan? You choose!

We all serve a purpose. Think of it this way. A character in a story doesn't tell the author what purpose they will serve. Therefore, once again, I ask us, who will we be, a "jar of treasure" or a "jar of trash"? God does not put His Spirit in "jars of trash"! God gives His gift of the Holy Spirit to those who are His friends, His children, the brethren of Jesus Christ. Always remember, the Holy Spirit is our best friend.

~ Chapter Six ~

PREPPING ESSENTIAL ME

Living without Labels

When I first started to get serious and submit to having a personal relationship with God, I learned one simple fact. This fact is not one of logic but I found that it remained true as I held to it in the development of my Christian walk. What I learned is that life is more about being refined than being defined.

As civilized people we are so comfortable with giving everything a name or label. It helps us to categorize which makes us feel in control. It's human nature for us to desire to be in control of our lives. However, as we continue to grow in God and develop a firm relationship with Him intimately, we begin to realize we're actually not in control of anything. This truth becomes easier to accept as time goes on and as we consistently maintain our communing with God.

Although we are God's children, we are human. As human beings, we normally want to continue to develop and reach higher heights in our personal lives. It's human nature to always want to be aware of our surroundings. This includes having at least an idea of the direction in life we're heading and knowing where we're at in life currently.

However, there will be times in life when we'll be unable to define who we are and where we're at; and further, who we will become. As we continue to develop in Christ we must adjust to the discomfort of not knowing from an intellectual perspective. To get a grip on faith sometimes we have to get adjusted to knowing without naturally knowing. This type of knowing is intimacy.

I heard long ago that "comfort can kill you." As Christian believers of this age, we've become so excited in this era in the church where vision and the ideal of "kingdom living" is dominating preached messages. Every time we go to church there's a "word" here or there. But what happens when what is happening in reality is not matching with what is being preached?

It's interesting to me how much God is speaking in the church. Yet we remain breached and corrupt. If all the modern "kingdom living" and "vision writing" messages that are being preached are really God driven, I don't think it would be a top priority considering the current state of the church. "The kingdom of God is within us, it cannot be detected with visible signs."

If we understand this, why do we subconsciously try to develop the Kingdom of God with our own "Kingdom living" theories? How can we, if Christ told us that the Kingdom of God is already here? As much as we say that we are "seeking the Kingdom of God and all its righteousness," we seem to actually be seeking a more prosperous life.

If you ask me, this prosperous lifestyle we deem "Kingdom living," seems to be very similar to what the world views as prosperity. There is nothing wrong with desiring a prosperous life, but God's perception of prosperity differs somewhat to mankind. God's perception of prosperity is both spiritual and natural but it starts on the inside before it manifest outwardly.

Spiritual Calling: Recollecting the Call

One of the most common things I've heard throughout my life is "God has something for you." You've probably heard the same, especially if you grew up in church. If you didn't grow up in the church, someone may have said something to you that reassured you internally that you're meant to do great things.

Some people refer to calling as prophecy and some others refer to calling as purpose. Other people may view calling as a promising career. I see it as God's calling for me "to will and to do His good pleasure." Further, I acknowledge it as M.O.R.E.: My Ordained Right to be Effective. No matter what we call the calling, it is recognized as a form of destiny that we feel is going to happen at some point in time.

It's like a tug on our hearts. It's a feeling that cannot be traced physically; yet it's felt without a doubt. It's a form of knowing that is not reasonable but intimate.

When it comes to our "calling" in God, we are already equipped with what we need. If we are not equipped, then in time, we will acquire whatever it is that we need to operate in the call. God does not call anybody to do anything without equipping them with what they need. When God calls us, He calls us with the intent of reaching others. Therefore, God must prepare and provide for us what we lack to perform the task.

God's calling to the individual person is like an echo that travels and captures the intended hearer attentive recognition. It also grabs the attention for others near to the intended hearer to become aware that a call has been made. When this happens two things will result: One, the person called and some near the person will gather to the voice. Two, the person called and some near the person will run away from the voice.

Either way, calling brings results and shifts people to and from one another. Anytime God speaks, changes and shifts always occur. This is a fact rather folk choose to acknowledge God's voice or not.

When God calls us, the calling will reveal who's really for us and who's not. This shows us who is of Christ and who's not. Those who accept the lifestyle of Christ are predestined to be called, justified, and glorified. This is the destiny of those God has already chosen for His purpose to be fulfilled on Earth.

The fact that we are predestined is why when we are called to do what God has destined us to do it doesn't seem to be a foreign experience. We feel right at home in the call. Naturally, we may have been taken totally by surprise, but spiritually we know that this "calling" is specifically for us. This knowing brings a potent sense of awareness in self and others.

People can always sense when God is on your life. Some people will fight God, and at the same time, fight you, because they fear the God in you- sinful guilt. Other people will cling to God, and at the same time, cling to you because they fear the God in you- reverence. Though they may not know Christ for themselves, they can discern the intimacy which attracts them to him through you.

Calling is a recollecting experience. The key to recalling God's call is to know His Word intimately over intellectually. One has to know they are being called in their heart and not by what they see.

I believe God gives us clues to what he is calling us to do for Him. However, I've learned the best way to transition peacefully in operating in our calling is by having an open, obedient, and willing heart to do what God calls us to do. This way, when God calls us into action we can accept what the call is for and be ready. Being ready for God's call has more to do with knowing Him intimately than what we know about Him intellectually.

Knowing

What does a person do when they don't know what to do? There are a few things. We can ask God and be still as we wait on Him. We can ask others for advice. We can even take matters into our own hands based upon what we think is best.

What I believe most people do is take matters into their own hands based upon what is thought to be best. In consideration of this, the question I want to present is, what does it mean to 'know' in terms of 'knowing' God? Can we fully know God? Can we ever come to a full understanding of God?

I believe we are indeed able to know God. However, while I believe this, I don't think that in this life we will be able to fully understand Him. God must be revealed to us through our belief and acceptance of Jesus Christ as our personal Lord and Savior. Similar to my thoughts of love by

God's standards, I believe knowing, as God views it, is a different perspective than ours as human beings.

I believe that knowing, as it relates to God, is a matter of intimacy opposed to a matter of intellect. Knowing, as it relates to God, cannot be determined by human reasoning. It is the intimate form of knowing that is pure and secure. This way of knowing is not able to be disproven: It cannot be formed totally through human logic.

Intimacy with God is not liable to the laws of human intellectual nature. Knowing God from the perspective of having a personal relationship with Him is being intimate with Him. This is a knowledge that is extremely important and necessary for our essential nature- our spiritual nature. Our essential nature is a combination of our heart, soul, mind, and strength. As followers of Christ and in order to obtain the kingdom of God that dwells within us, Christ instructs us "to love God with all of these- heart, soul, mind, and strength." These four are the essential immeasurable portions of who we are.

I believe that truly knowing God is in the heart, and only He, who alone knows the heart, knows those who truly know Him. "But God's truth stands firm like a foundational stone with this inscription: "The Lord knows those who are His," and "All who belong to the Lord must turn away from evil (2 Timothy 2:19 NLT)."

Knowing God intimately is having a solid foundation of belief in Him in our hearts. I've found that the mind can play games, and the lips can speak lies. However, the heart, while it definitely can deceive us, it has a difficult time lying on itself. The heart has a mind of its own and lips to speak on its own accord. The solution to our heart problem is to put our hearts in God's hands. We do this by denying ourselves and obeying God's Word. This gives us a firm foundation to stand on and be confident in knowing God and His truth- Jesus Christ.

It is difficult to have a solid foundation in Jesus without knowing Him for ourselves through our study of God's Word. The Word is what secures us in confidently knowing God. However, knowing the content of the Bible does not mean anything if one does not allow the Word to settle and take root in the heart.

While many people may read the Bible and know well its content, they do not hear it spiritually in their hearts. Therefore, they lack the true understanding of it that only comes from the Holy Spirit whom only comes through relationship with Jesus. I think that as many of us say we know and live the Bible, this is not the case, based upon the content of our character.

Character is a mirrored reflection of the heart. It amazes me how many people claim to follow Jesus and yet their character proves otherwise. As disciples of Jesus, our character should mirror his love. This is most effective when we show Jesus' love toward our fellow disciples. As followers of Jesus Christ "The world will know us based upon our love for one another. (John 13:35)"

I believe this is referring to mainly fellow believers opposed to the world. Reverend Timothy Ruffin stated that "being spiritual and being stupid are two different things." How can we be so sweet and patient to non-Christians and be so sour and judgmental toward our fellow Christian brothers and sisters?

Some non-believers have no intention to accept Jesus Christ and are just looking for handouts. One must have discernment even in serving to compel the nations (see John 6:24-29). The point is to compel the lost in the world to know God through Jesus Christ.

Knowing God and His Word truly, is not a reflection of our knowledge of the Word but the change that takes place in us. The Bible in simple ways is a story of God's character shown by His love for the world by the effort He has made to restore us. Listening to what the Bible says doesn't just take reading it, it takes applying it into our lives. However, listening to what the Bible says also takes having a will to hear and obey. "He that has an ear let him hear- let him listen and understand."

How many of us have an ear to listen and understand the Bible with a heart set on learning it to learn God for ourselves? Having a heart set to know who God is for ourselves takes having a love for God. Knowing God is proven in our love for God. Our love for God is shown by our obedience to Him. It's hard to obey God without seeking Him, and that takes spending time with Him, getting to know Him through His Son in the Word by His Spirit, and praying without ceasing.

Keeping ourselves open to God intimately in every aspect of our lives allows us to truly know God. I believe that this intimacy comes with more knowledge of who God is because being fully open to God is the action showing that we want to know Him better heart to heart. We can only know God heart to heart through the intimate knowledge of Jesus Christ. Becoming identical with Christ is proof that we actually know God for ourselves.

~ Chapter Seven ~

WE, THE PEOPLE

Family Matters

The one practical thing I've learned about life as time goes by is that people, places, and things change. So of course it's not hard to understand that as these things change family will easily change. In all honesty, my own family has experienced dramatic change over the last few years. This has led me to write about the dynamics of families in society as it relates to God.

Family matters, but as of late, family hasn't seemed to matter to people as it should. The only thing thicker than blood is our relationship with the Holy Spirit. The Holy Spirit should be the center of family dynamics. When we lack acknowledgement of the Holy Spirit we lose focus of what it takes to maintain the spirit of family. By losing focus of what it takes to maintain the spirit of family, the family becomes unattached at its core root.

"You can't help who you're born to!" This is a statement that my cousin Damian has said time and time again. It seems that people choose who they want as family opposed to accepting the family that God has placed them with. People have done this for reasons of embarrassment, anger, molestation, abuse, etc. Despite any reason, it all comes down to the negative spiritual components that are affecting families today.

No other family has been affected by spiritual wickedness than the average low-income urban black family. In American society alone, the deterioration of the black family is clear to see. We can see this clearly by considering the average urban black home.

The average black home is not a family with a single mother making $30,000 or more with a car, and a job in nursing. The average black family is the family that is on the border line of total brokenness and separation. These families are barely making it through, having to do just about anything to survive, and opportunity is almost not an option. For the average black person, in the average black home, in the average black family in America, opportunity to be better seems rare.

The system never seems to work for black people and that is because it wasn't designed for black people. Knowing this to be true, how can the average black person, who will lead the average black family, become successful and break this chain? How does the average black person stay true to their self without being conformed in their pursuit for better? The answer is by being centered in Christ by depending upon God's Word. This keeps our minds fixed on Jesus.

When our minds are fixed on Jesus in all our endeavors we are given direction by the Holy Spirit. Black families require the Holy Spirit in order to make it. It is a matter of life or death for us. Because the dynamics of families are not centered in Jesus we are easily corrupted in our pursuits. Families have become so wrapped up in the norm of culturally deemed success that we've forgotten about God.

We now groom our families, and worse, our children, to go after the tangible things of this world. I believe this is wrong either way because "in all our ways we are to acknowledge God". Our reverence for God despite our triumphs and trials is what keeps us aligned with Him.

When we don't depend on Jesus we are not aligned with God. When we're not aligned with God we're not on accord with Him. As a result, we're out of order naturally because we're out of order spiritually. Families are out of order today because they are void of the Holy Spirit. This results in people not acknowledging God in everything, including the dynamics of family.

If the family is not on one accord spiritually, there is no unity because the family is essentially not in agreement at its core root. The family must have a solid foundation in Christ, making the Holy Spirit the common factor that relates them. It is the Holy Spirit that unites us and keeps us united on one accord with God as a unit. This unifies the family, the home, the person, and makes a nation truly "one nation under God, indivisible, with liberty and justice for all."

In God Do We Trust?

In much respect, America, in my opinion, has never really reverenced God. It has been often said that America was built on Christian principles. In addition, statistically,

Christianity is considered the dominant religion in America. In my opinion, the foundation of the United States is not grounded upon Christian principles but rather the convenience of it.

In order for something to be built upon a principle it must hold to the standards of that principle. America does not hold to the standard of Christianity because the standard of Christianity is Jesus Christ. Since Jesus is the embodiment of the living Word of God and he is not honored correctly in this nation, America cannot sincerely be a nation that is built on Christian principles.

In fact, I pose to us that money and academic education is more honored and glorified in America than God. When one considers black slavery in America, I don't believe Christian principles fit into the picture. Even the freeing of black slaves was more about financial convenience than Christian conscience.

Sometimes the best way to get what one wants, in a spiritually corrupt world, is to tolerate with what one hates: In my opinion, in this case, it was tolerating the freedom of black slaves. I think America chose what it considered the lesser of two evils in order to profit from what this country loves most-money. A sinful mind will put up with what it hates to satisfy its desires. This is a trait similar to addiction.

America needs to recover by being reborn in Christ. Like other great nations that were reformed in God's standards, including Rome, America proudly claims to be a nation formed in God's standards. Yet America fails to truly abide in the standard of Christianity- Jesus Christ. America only acknowledges God by word of mouth and not in heart. Our nation is indeed great but we require heavy repentance.

America has its good, but it's the bad that bothers me. We can be a very wicked nation, and its wicked ways are clear forms of Satanic influence. A people make a nation and form its culture. The culture of America has become truly parallel with Satan's character.

We proclaim the glory and righteousness of the red, white, and blue, but all the while, we are thinking, living, and breathing money green. Similarly, our nation's claim to be "one nation under God," along with our false motto "In God We Trust," is a great deception. The actual god that America trust in is money. By the same token, the only doctrine we believe in and study is academia. I believe that in order for us to truly be "one nation under God, indivisible," America has to repent.

How do we do this? Well, I see four things we must do specifically. All four are impossible to do without a change of heart. The first thing we ought to do as a nation is humble ourselves before God. Secondly, we must pray to God for forgiveness and ask consistently for guidance. Third, we must seek God's face, acknowledging him in all our ways. Fourth, we must turn from our wicked ways in total repentance.

Unfortunately, I'm not confident in this happening before it's too late. Perhaps, if we do this individually maybe one day a standard truly set and built on Christian principles will challenge this nation to see the error of its ways and become better.

America is not a house built on a solid foundation and because of this we are beginning to waver. We've already been blown away in our faith. However, God is able to use a remnant of His people to turn the hearts and minds of people in America back to Him.

Divinely Insensitive

I think people in society today are becoming very emotionally insensitive toward their consideration of other people. However, despite how emotionally insensitive people can be toward others, they seem to be more emotionally sensitive to themselves. Today, we are so into self-health and self-care that it seems we are forgetting about caring for one another in general. People are becoming so wrapped up in themselves as they conform to the norm that is deemed appropriate and acceptable by society.

We live in an era in society where we verbally elevate freedom of self-expression. However, when we see self-expression bringing about conviction we shun those people. People claim to be in favor of standing out, but when someone stands out for the sake of holiness, we persecute them for not remaining reserved for their comfort.

Society is comfortable with people being unique as long as it doesn't convict for Godly change. Yes, anyone can be themselves as long as they can be controlled. Is controlling who a person is, allowing that person to truly be free? I find that society fears an individual whose demeanor convicts with a godliness. This is because society is Satanically influenced and has become an enemy of God.

We exist in a society consumed in fear. I also believe that fear has caused society to linger in ungodly pride, selfishness, and jealousy which are opposing attributes of God's image and likeness.

Human beings are not designed by God to be prideful, selfish, or jealous. These attributes are self-centered traits that are the result of our corrupt nature as beings made in love. We corrupt our essential nature by leaning to our own understanding, contradicting God's Word, and compromising God's will for our lives.

It seems the more knowledgeable people are becoming about themselves, the more ignorant they are becoming about God. More and more we deny the Holy Spirit and we place our confidence in ourselves. It is society's profanity before God that is causing people to become more like robots than human beings.

It appears that human emotion is becoming less naturally sociable as many people have disconnected from God. We must reconnect with God because He is the source of what makes us human. We are made in God's image and likeness. How could God not be the source of humanity if it started with Him in the first place?

The main problem today is the ignorance of the Holy Spirit among people. The Holy Spirit is God, who is not only the source of true love, but He is love by love's essential and initial identity. As the acknowledgement of the Holy Spirit is decreasing in society, so also is love.

As love decreases in society, faith also decreases. As faith is decreasing in society, so is our obedience to will and to do God's good pleasure in our lives to believe in His Son, Jesus Christ, and to be light in a dark world. People who carry Christ within them are the light that is left in this world.

However, as some Christians are conforming to the norms of society, it seems like the light in this world is dimming. I feel that we have become successful in developing a logical society as we live by facts, falsifiable theories, and tangible evidence. This is even becoming a fact within the church.

I believe that the faith people have in themselves void out the fear of God, causing people to reject their need of Christ. Society rejects Jesus and are being conditioned in a society that is reprobate in itself and becoming more lost.

People disown the discipline of faith by not obeying the Word of God and not submitting to God's will.

~ Chapter Eight ~

LIVING AN INTANGIBLE TANGIBLE LIFE

Living Disconnected

Have you ever felt alone despite being in a room filled with people? I've felt this way my entire life, living as a black Christian male in America. In fact, often, I still feel this way. However, it's no longer a fear of mine, but it's now a strange love affair. It's an affair of security despite an uncomfortable sense of exposure: It's a spiritually awkward feeling along with a proud and refreshing sensation of truth.

This sensation is similar to being aware that everyone around you can see your private parts in broad day light. But the sensation is absent of shame despite the sense of awareness. Forgive me for the description, but this is how I feel, standing out as a follower of Jesus Christ. I'd be lying if I said that I felt I was the only believer feeling this way, when truthfully, I know that I'm not.

However, please don't confuse living disconnected spiritually from society to be something negative, as this is not the case. Living disconnected spiritually from society is the lifestyle of one who sanctifies God (Isaiah 8:13) in a society engulfed in Satan's influence. To the unbeliever, this sounds crazy, but to the believer who knows Christ intimately, this is a reality.

As believers, we live in a world where Satan's mentality and attributes rule and run rapid among those not saved. The Holy Spirit by way of the blood of Jesus Christ is who protects believers in a society heavily under Satan's influence. The Holy Spirit is the living water that flows within believers, keeping us alert in the truth. The flow of the Holy Spirit satisfies and nourishes believers as we are the light in a society in darkness.

The darkness of society keeps people blind to the truth. The truth is the same as the light. The light is the lifestyle that God desires for us to live as his chosen elect. Believers must always live in the light to give vision to those who cannot see.

People linger blindly in the darkness of society. Those who live in this darkness of falsehoods and deceptions their entire lives get used to living in lies. To them, the life they live is not of lies but rather the only life they know.

However, knowing the Holy Spirit intimately changes this perception. Knowing the Holy Spirit intimately allows one to see things as they really are without boundaries and the excessive need of human logic. This knowing causes us to be confident and secure in God's Word. It also empowers us to live up to God's standard which keeps us secure. This security is in Jesus Christ.

Christ is the Word of God as well as God Himself. This is not something that can be explained to folk who do not wish to accept this in their hearts. It is the confidence that one obtains after receiving Jesus. Living for Christ is more about being than knowing. This is the best advice I can give to someone struggling with Christianity. Christ is the integrity that believers have, causing us to live set apart from the darkness.

The Benefit of Knowing God

Growing up, my Mom taught me a simple prayer. It was a part of the morning devotion that my sister and I said with her before leaving for school and work. The part in the prayer was, "Lord, give us eyes to see you; ears to hear you; a heart, soul, spirit, and mind to obey, love, and praise you". Those words set up our entire day in that they were reverential in acknowledging our need of God throughout the day.

Honestly, it has been a long time since my mother, sister, and I have prayed in the morning together. This is because many changes have taken place: marriage, children, living location, jobs, age; you know, the everyday grown up things. However, those habitual morning prayers we said taught me the importance of praying daily. We may need to get better as praying as a family again, but at least we all continue to pray individually. We at least maintained the habit of praying. Nevertheless, I believe families should pray together, unifying physically as well as spiritually.

I believe this is what's wrong with families and individuals today. We don't pray! Therefore, we have no direction from God. God is not only our director, God is our direction. When we pray in Jesus' name, we acknowledge the truth that Jesus Christ is the way of God's direction.

The Bible tells us that "in Christ we live, move, and have our being." It also tells us that "we are nothing without God." This is a truth that people in society fail to acknowledge. Literally, nothing we do and nothing we are can be without God. Yet, we fail to act on this knowledge of God in our existence.

We are made in the image and likeness of God which is made through the image and likeness of Christ. So why deny Christ? If we deny Christ we might as well deny ourselves: Christ is the source of who we are and how we came into being.

The ignorance of Christ is what causes society to be unstable. We blindly think we have control in this world by our human intelligence. However, one basic rule applies in human intelligence and that is, "nothing from nothing is nothing." It is logically impossible to get something out of nothing. The only way to get something out of nothing is through something divine.

As human beings, we exist as fragments in time. People have a habit of needing reason or logic for everything.

It is an unspoken truth that anything we fail to see reason or logic in is not worthy of purpose. This mentality causes us to limit ourselves in even what we consider progress in knowledge.

When we operate in life based on limitations, we limit our God given potential in life. While we live, we have to operate in our lives as God purposed us. Once we die it's too late. Many people fail to live a full life according to God's plan because we choose our own plan: Thereby, we live, move, and have being based upon our own understanding of ourselves. Living according to our own definition for our lives limits us because we didn't create ourselves.

It is human nature for us to define the moments of our lives because it helps us feel like we're in control. But how can we be in control of a world, not to mention an entire Universe of worlds that we probably will never fully understand in a lifetime? A good number of people in society today can't even understand who they are themselves, and some of these people have been living for thirty years or more.

Some will never understand themselves because they are too busy going through life seeking a definition of themselves that they don't understand. Only God has the right answer to who we really are and where we're at in life. He holds the fullness of our potential that we have yet to realize. Because some people fail to acknowledge God, they fail to realize the true potential that He has given them.

One reason why people won't acknowledge God is because some folk are selfish by nature. They are selfish because of fear. People are so fearful of things not going their way. They're so worried that things won't go the way they planned. Therefore, they commit their own lives to their own methods, motives, and mentality.

The root of being totally devoted to self without God is ungodly pride. "But pride comes before a fall." Sometimes it's best to fall at some point. It's best for us to stumble on God's Word. In this we are proven imperfect and vulnerable. This leaves us open for God to show His strength in our weakness.

Most people find imperfection and vulnerability to be pillars of insecurity. But for those who are dependent upon Christ, these pillars are landmarks of security in God. This takes losing yourself to find yourself anew in God through Christ. In God is where one finds unlimited power and potential. In God we are able to see beyond the momentum of each moment we are granted in our lives with unlimited possibilities. This is a start of finding the Kingdom of God that already dwells in us.

Don't lose the Fire

In a world that makes common sense for common cents, faith is something we all struggle with today. In my opinion, the fire of the human spirit is almost all the way out among mankind. Some people might as well be machines as their hearts, minds, and essentially, their total being has adapted to the nature of this technological age of modern society that is led by logic.

Technology is the tool and weapon we use to battle human digression. Our progress in technology has made life a lot quicker, and for some, it has made life a lot easier. However, technology does not take into account the spiritual heart, as it thrives off of the logical rule- "Only the strong survive." This rule abandons the value of love, the presence of faith, and the importance of hope. All three are intangible factors that cause humanity to remain humane.

Technology was designed to help society to progress not lead society in its progression toward an evolved class of humanity. It seems the keeper of mankind's existence has been taken out of the hands of the Creator and into the hands of the created. Anything man made is still in the hands of man, and is under man's control. Sin causes people to desire control of their own lives in every aspect.

The point of all this is to present an ideal of why people are losing this fire known as the human spirit. The human spirit is void without the presence of the Holy Spirit. We give ourselves too much credit and present too many theories about what it takes to be united as one people: "One nation under God, indivisible, with liberty and justice for all."

For Americans, this clause alone is the answer of how we can obtain true unity in this nation. However, how can we be "One nation under God," and "indivisible" when we do not have justice for all? Also, how can we be "One nation under God" if we are rejecting Jesus Christ?

According to the Bible, "No man comes to God, the Father accept through Jesus Christ- the Son of God." Therefore, we void out the proclaimed "foundation" of this country by our own contradiction in our pledge to the nation. Truthfully, the United States has never been "one nation". Instead, we have in fact, been divisible from the very founding of this country. If you don't believe me look at the series of events concerning racism, inequality, and poverty throughout the years of our great land's existence.

We have never been intact as a people. Now the anger of those in America is colliding with the ungodly pride of ungodly leaders governing this country. This is causing America to begin to collapse from the inside out. A wild fire has been blazing in this country, and that fire is a fury that is beginning to engulf the nation on both sides. My words are only a spec compared to people who are stepping out by voice and action: Besides, it's nothing that this nation hasn't seen before, only a different form and generation.

The fire of the Holy Spirit is now decreasing in American society, and throughout the world. The decrease of the fire of the Holy Spirit is what is allowing the United States to crumble. God is a "consuming fire," and His fire sets all things ablaze that it touches. When God's consuming fire sets an object ablaze, one of two things will result in His consumption. The object set ablaze will move into action and burn up whatever it touches, or either the object will stand still ablaze, and won't touch anything, and be consumed completely by the fire, and consumed into nothing, leaving it a desolate ruin.

No matter the result, consumption shall take place. God's fire cannot be extinguished rather it be His fury or His fullness. God's fire always contains His passion. God's passion is always the fullness of His Word. One receives the fire one way or another. It would be wise to burn with His fullness opposed to burning with His fury. Reverence of the Holy Spirit seems to be decreasing in this world because people are rejecting Jesus Christ. We are rejecting God's spirit by choice. In our rejection of the Holy Spirit we lose intangible and unified peace, joy, and happiness.

This peace, joy, and happiness, that the Holy Spirit gives us is unable to be touched. Therefore the peace, joy, and happiness, we get from the Holy Spirit is unable to be broken within us. The peace, joy, and happiness we get from the Holy Spirit become our security. They are the result of placing and keeping our integrity and dignity in God.

A Method to Living

I remember speaking to a co-worker of mine after we left a training. The conversation was generally about people and the state of this world. Based on the conversations I have had with my co-worker, I know that he knew of Jesus Christ, but I don't believe he was saved. I would continue to speak to him often, in order to plant seeds, with the hope that prayerfully one day these seeds will fall on fertile soil in his heart and that he will be saved.

We agreed that spirituality in this world has a role in society, but is often rejected, neglected, and ignored. We also agreed on how much this world has turned a blind eye to what is truly important in this life, and that spiritual warfare is clearly starting to take physical form in modern society. As we talked, it amazed me of how there were so many people in Center City Philadelphia who looked so secure and carefree by worldly standards, and yet they looked lifeless: You could see it in their faces. There wasn't a sincere continence in their facial expressions, and it was as if they were oblivious to what life is really about.

For me, this experience of observation and conversation served as a spiritual look at the blueprint of the society we live in today. It's sad! There are so many people who are walking around chasing success in this life and they find only the benefits of it. People like this find success and bask in its benefits and experience much in life, yet they never really find out what life is really all about.

They are dead on the inside. Not all of them, just a good portion. They chase, and are willing to sacrifice much of almost everything for this temporary life. This is actually a good method of attitude to be willing to lose everything to gain more. However, the wrong method can ruin the right motive. By the same token, the wrong motive can spoil the right method. The result is a dead life. A life dead to what is really essential in life. I've found that what's really essential and fulfilling about life is life itself.

Now some may say, "Well, that's what people are doing- living life." Some others may actually think about it and understand that the life we live is not all about just what we share or experience, but more importantly, how we live it. There is a certain way, a correct way, a right method of living life.

Living like we only live once is a lie. This is not the right method of living, but rather a deceptive way. Our young generation is led by a motto/method in how to live. This motto/method is known as the (YOLO) lifestyle, meaning "You Only Live Once." But we actually don't only live once.

We live twice! Death is just a checkpoint to continue on to our essential life- our spiritual/eternal life.

Today's society views this (YOLO) method of living as ambition. However, this mindset of living is specifically ambiguous to our youth, even to the part of the nation that are living the Word of God amiss. In Christ we have eternal life. However, according to the Bible, even without Christ we live on, but we live on in Hell- eternal damnation. We must be born again in the Spirit.

After living life any way we desire, without a relationship with Jesus, we may get what we desire in this physical life, but we lose our lives spiritually. By living after our physical nature only, we waste our choice to live according to our essential spiritual nature. When we choose to live by our spiritual nature, we choose to live up to the potential of the greatest portion of who we are in God. We are spiritual beings by God's original design of us.

Our potential in God is limitless, because God has created us in His image and likeness through Jesus, who is also limitless. We are created by limitless potential so that we can live by limitless potential. This way, we can also exemplify limitless potential. God is limitless potential. Yet we fail to acknowledge this spiritual gift of potential and cling to our physical potential and physical desires.

We waste the essential potential of our spiritual nature because we don't believe who we are. We don't believe in who we are because we don't know who we are. We don't know who we are because we don't know where we come from. We don't know where we come from because we don't know who we come from. We don't know who we come from because we choose not to believe in the embodiment of who we come from. The embodiment of who we come from is Jesus Christ.

Christ sent us the Holy Spirit to assure us of the truth, and Jesus Christ himself, is the truth. The Holy Spirit is the Spirit of God the Father. Jesus Christ and God the Father are one as the Bible teaches us. Therefore, if Christ is one with God the Father, and the Holy Spirit is the Spirit of God the Father, then Christ is also one with the Holy Spirit- hence the Trinity.

As we reject, neglect, and choose to ignore the Holy Spirit, we do the same to the gift of Jesus Christ. In turn, we insult God by rejecting the gift of the Holy Spirit that Christ sent, because Christ received the Holy Spirit from God the Father to give to us freely. The Holy Spirit is our direct connection to God the Father that comes through Jesus Christ. So if we blaspheme the Holy Spirit we disrespect our direct connection to God.

The Holy Spirit is our connection that is needed to assure us of who we are in God. The Holy Spirit is the gift that advocates for us, and is the bridge of our refinement in God.

Refinement in God has divine essential purpose. Divine essential purpose is what society lacks. People live amiss of who they are when they have no sense of purpose. Divine essential purpose is our true purpose that is directly related and connected to who we are called to be.

People with no awareness of who they are essentially live life amiss their actual potential. They die full and not empty, leaving the life they left behind unfulfilled. An unfulfilled life affects the lives that are connected to us. We never know who we are destined to influence spiritually. No one can know for sure who God has assigned to them. I've found that always being aware of the potential influence we have in God is key to living life on purpose. Our assignment to others is more essential than we give credit because everyone has a purpose to fulfill for God's plan.

I think that when we die, we should die empty of life. In other words we should die feeling fulfilled. We can never know for sure, but because of this fact, I think it is important to see things to the end. "Finishing is better than starting. Patience is better than pride (Ecclesiastes 7:8 NLT)."

I sometimes think of my life as a cup, stacked up in its place among a pyramid of other cups with Christ life at the top. With each breath, and each second we live on Earth, our cups are being filled. As our lives progress, our cups of life are being filled with each moment. What we are being filled with in life runs over into other cups of life connected to us.

This is how our lives in Christ should work. With each moment, our lives should come to a point where it is constantly being filled, overflowing into the people around us. We don't have to know other people to pour into their cups (their lives). All we have to do is be in the position that God has placed us, and man our position well. We also have to keep our connection open and remain sincere with God in spirit and in truth, by just "being" in God.

We cannot "be" in God if we are being defined by others or ourselves. Being defined in life causes us to put caps on the cups of our lives. As a result, we cannot receive or give what we gain in life. We must be refined, remaining open to receive and ready to give. This is living life on purpose, for a purpose, by a purpose. We should live a full life in Christ to empty out our cups so that someone else can exceed their full potential and eventually become empty when their cup is also required by God. We die empty by loving as God has loved us.

Fading to Black: God or Us

At some point, we all have to come to a place in life where we must choose either God or ourselves. This is a difficult choice for us to make as the choice is a battle within us. It takes work to choose God over ourselves, and it is a daily battle. This war has the potential to take our lives. However, we already have the victory through receiving Jesus Christ.

Todays society lacks faith in God. While this generation doesn't lack spirituality, it is engulfed in various spiritual practices. Today, people are all about expression. Expression comes in various forms. People love to express themselves in their own way. It's a form of "escapism."

We escape reality in our expression of beliefs, and in our choices, because we desire to feel free. Feeling free is the closest sensation we have to feel like we're in control. Despite all efforts to be in control, we know intimately that we are not in control, and will never truly be.

The positive dark side, that is the source of this era of spirituality and expression, is the passion of people. Society is becoming more passionate and sensitive about what they feel individually. The problem with this is that fear is what this era of society feels most.

America is engulfed in fear. Our nation is slave to the shadows, bound by our choice to remain blind to the truth. "Truth always brings closure and produces disclosure."

The United States deals with the dirt we choose to deal with on the surface, but fails to deal with the dirt originating from under our dirty foundation. As a result of not dealing with the dirt, our own people are left struggling. Those who struggle the most are the people who have always struggled since the country's foundation. No other people in the United States of America struggle more than the average low income African American family.

The scary part is that some African Americans will argue this truth and try to point out things that will justify why black folk struggle in this country. Everything has a starting point. America has played a huge part concerning the condition black people currently exist in. How does a people whose origin comes from a continent of natural wealth and a rich history- shown by both Biblical and historical perspectives, become so oppressed and degraded worldwide?

Despite "the struggle" among black Americans, we have survived. However, the issue is that though we survive, we are still left unsatisfied. For all we are, considering what we have endured, we are counted as the least of humanity.

We are viewed as inferior all around the world. This is because out of all people on this Earth we fail to remain true to who we really are as a whole. We have lost almost all sense of who we really are essentially. Black folk by nature are not a people that can be defined by history, man-made laws, or statistics. We fail and come short of all these things that define a people.

Black people worldwide are a people of no distinct definition. We are a spiritual people that can only be labeled in refinement. Therefore, we are unable to be defined distinctively, because we are always adaptable. We have proven to be a people who by nature are able to adjust in any circumstance.

Unfortunately, today, we are losing our will to adapt more and more. As we adapt away from our sincere relationship with God, and ignore our belief in Jesus Christ, we adjust away from who we really are in God. Who we are in God is our essential nature.

Our true identity in God is a people of faith, integrity, mobility, and endurance. These attributes do not exist in us without God. Without God we essentially lose our identity.

African Americans have lost their identity because we have become bitter from our oppressed state. Further, we have become ignorant of our reverence and knowledge of God. In fact, due to our misplaced blame, I believe some of us actually have come to hate God. This is a danger zone for African Americans and any people like this. The Bible tells us, "All who hate God, love death."

Today, people in the United States label and view the church as irrelevant, foolish, and hypocritical. Sadly, this is only the beginning as considering the state of humanity in the book of Revelation in the Bible. There is still a spiritual war raging, and it is beginning to manifest physically. America is smack dab in the middle of it all.

Considering the spiritual state African Americans are in, we are in a bad position. We're not even in the best position as a people physically or mentally either.

African Americans today are very passionate about the progress that we feel we deserve, given our history in this country. During the Civil Rights movement the black church was the main source of the progress our people have made toward change. Back then we had true unity as a people because we were on one accord with God. We allowed God to lead us, and we held to His standard.

During the Civil Rights movement Black pride was at a pure all-time high. We may not have had much knowledge of our physical origin but we were aware of who we were spiritually. This even drew other races to support us, and this was because the spirit of the cause was led by the Holy Spirit.

The difference between then and now was the reverence of the standard driven by the Holy Spirit. Often, we acknowledge our leaders as educated Black men and women. We don't acknowledge enough that although most of them were educated or pursuing an education, most had a foundation and dedication to the church. Our black leaders back then were people of God who had a foundation in Christ which allowed them to be leaders of a standard of faith, integrity, mobility, and endurance despite adversity.

Today, the standard of our foundation is acknowledged and built upon mostly education. At some point educational honors has overlapped our God ordained humility. Academia has taken the lead position over our God and has become our foundational source of our faith, integrity, mobility and endurance. We have surrendered our God given sense for common cents. Although the world wants us to believe that we are common people, truth is, we are not, not even by nature.

However, we have accepted commonality, thrown away God, and abandoned our God given sense. It bothers me how many of our people are speaking up with true passion for our people, yet they are ignorantly fatigued of praying to God. Some have even claimed prayer to be foolish in the sense that “it doesn't work for our people anymore.”

What's scary about this is that their theories sound good to us, whereas, the church is sounding worse as time goes by. "In all our ways we are to acknowledge God and He will direct our path." Due to our anger, as a result of our impatience, and the fact that we are lost in ourselves, this has caused us to believe we can "save" ourselves.

Could it be we have fallen into American culture so much spiritually that we too desire to be our own God? Have we become a people with more love and reverence for each other, than our love and reverence for God? God is still a jealous God. He has still allowed us to be here despite the attempts of other people (racism) and our own attempts to wipe us out (for example black on black violence).

Perhaps this uproar of our true passion due to the world's oppression of us is God's way of revealing to us the truth of our hearts toward Him? Sadly, the people are too angry to say Amen, and many black churches are too busy shouting to stop and instead be a light for our people.

Satisfying Fulfillment

Like many, for years, I have searched for satisfaction in life: The satisfaction that nourishes my entire being. Throughout my life I have had a thirst for thorough completion. This "thorough completion" is a sense of fulfillment that is physically impossible to obtain.

The hard truth that I had to adjust my mind to is that it is impossible for any human being to find this true satisfaction without God. Yet I found good news in knowing that "with God all things are possible".

All over the world, people seek satisfaction in people, places, and things. Awkwardly, society presents even people to us. People are more esteemed by other people. In fact, people formulate their own identity from the influence of other people. People have become our own motivation, and we mirror our own image among ourselves. Being our own motivation and mirroring our own image is what places us out of alignment with God.

As a result, we formulate our own identity out of the corrupt urge to define ourselves. I've learned that there is no satisfaction in defining ourselves alone, because definition comes with limitation. Definition is what is used to be logically definite in understanding who we are.

It is human nature to want to be confident in knowing who we are. However, I find defining our true identity to be something that we cannot distinctively accomplish because of the simple fact of change. In every moment that we live, we are always changing. We change as the world changes, along with every experience, and form of knowledge we gain. The inability to be immune to what we are aware of is what changes people. We can choose to ignore what we are aware of, but the truth is, awareness remains, rather we choose to acknowledge it or not.

How can we define ourselves when we are constantly changing as we become more aware? Even experience and observation plays a role in grooming a human being to become different. With every extension of our awareness we are challenged to inevitably grow. In fact, we are pushed by the intangible force of awareness to grow. Some people choose not to change. This is ignorance by way of fear: the deliberate ignorance to move despite being naturally moved. Deliberate ignorance is a form of spiritual arrogance birthed through fear.

As we deliberately ignore the spiritual instinct to move toward change, we automatically reject fulfillment. For example, family members who choose to not speak to one another out of anger of an issue, causing negative tension within the family, which in turn may keep certain family members from interacting with each other comfortably. This is an example of deliberately ignoring to move toward fulfillment that is being pushed by the spiritual instinct of reaching a settled matter.

Once again, there is a method to living, and life is empty when rejecting fulfillment. People need fulfillment. There is not a single day that a human being lives when they do not instinctively and intuitively have a need. It is human nature to need and to desire fulfillment in our needs. Our needs are physical, mental, and spiritual. Each need desires fulfillment. There is no instinctive and intuitive need for fulfillment greater than a need for fulfillment.

Have you ever had an itch you couldn't scratch? If you scratch it, you find not only relief but a sense of fulfilled comfort. Now imagine an itch that you know is there, and may even know exactly where it is. However, when you scratch it, you can't seem to relieve yourself and receive fulfillment. This type of itch is what it's like searching for spiritual satisfaction. The only way to fulfill this itch is to go to the source of who we are, and that source is Jesus Christ. This is why it is important to learn who we are in Christ.

Learning who we are in Jesus Christ is essential if we want to obtain satisfaction in who we are essentially. The Bible tells us in John 1, "In the beginning was the Word, and the

Word was with God, and the Word was God." We learn that Jesus Christ is the Word in the flesh, and we also learn in this same chapter, that "everything that was made on this Earth was made through Jesus Christ." Jesus Christ for us is the "prototype." It is in the image and likeness of Jesus Christ, that men and women were all created. Therefore, if we want fulfillment and relief in our lives, we need the source.

Christ tells us in John 14 that "we can ask for anything in his name, and he will do it, so that he, the Son of God, can bring glory to God the Father." All we have to learn to do is ask for things in accordance to God's will. Jesus Christ and His Father are one. So when we ask for satisfaction it should be in accordance to God's will for our lives. We find out what God's will is for our lives in His Word.

~ Chapter Nine ~

THE CHURCH IN THE WILD

Spirit and Truth

The Bible tells us that "God is a spirit, and those who worship Him must worship Him in spirit and in truth". I believe that the significance of one's spirit lies in the essential nature of who one is. The significance of truth is that it is pure. What makes truth pure is that it is sincere. In order for one to worship God in spirit and in truth by His standards, I believe one has to worship Him in the essence and in the sincerity of who they really are. Therefore, for example, if one is angry with God they should respectfully communicate the sincere details of why they are angry with Him.

Could it be that some of God's people in the church are worshiping Him from a false place within? Could this also affect how we compel those who are lost in coming to know the truth about who God is and what He's about? I have found that some people display and exemplify themselves falsely before God. Perhaps this is because the exemplified worship of some people is not a sincere display of who they really are. Who we really are is who we are essentially.

This leads me to question if we know who we really are? I don't think a good portion of us do. People spend so much time perfecting the practice of man-made church standards. This has led some people to do things on their own without God, ultimately being at odds with or leaving the church. I believe some believers are falling short in exhibiting the standards of God that Jesus Christ has exemplified for us to mirror.

Worship can be exhibited in many forms. I have found that the beauty of worshiping God is not as attractive as human beings think. In fact, I pose to us that worship that is done in spirit and in truth can get ugly. Worship can physically be a nasty sight because of the battle of perspectives between the spirit and the flesh that takes place within people. However, it is beautiful to God when we look at the spiritual and truthful side of it all.

The road to true deliverance can be ugly physically, tough mentally, but beautiful spiritually. I've learned that when developing a relationship with God, and growing in the relationship, the breakdown is more important than the break through. Some of us fail to see ourselves fulfilled in the breakthrough because we miss the point that the breakdown was supposed to teach us. Consider Jesus' victory on the cross: Christ's entire experience on the cross, although physically, it was a messy process that was viewed by some as Christ's failure; spiritually, in God's point of view, the experience was a majestic process of victory.

Some churches in today's society have simply become nothing more than "branches of religious social organizations." Like a lot of social organizations, some churches are no longer fond with "getting their hands dirty," serving real issues. In order to change this, believers must not be afraid to show people the scars of their sinful past. What happened to the believer that is not afraid to expose the truth about their scared life before being transformed by the convicting power of the Holy Spirit?

Similar to Paul in the Bible, we have to remember to be "glad to boast about our weaknesses, so that the power of

Christ can work through us." We are effective in compelling people in spirit and in truth by allowing them to see the entire truth about who we are, and not only the truth of who we are now. Exposure is what breaks down barriers. Exposure is what shows the truth.

How can the world believe in the truth of Jesus Christ if we hide the truth about ourselves? Some believers hide their true selves from other people just as easily as they think they hide their true selves from God. I think that believers have perfected their practice of "church going" more than perfecting the practice of continuing to edify the body of Christ as the community of believers the church is actually supposed to be.

We shouldn't be a community that is divided by different denominations and practices. Some church congregations have developed a distorted identity of the church- the Body of Christ. I believe that this is because we spend more time becoming perfect by the standards of church politics and image than we spend trying to become perfect by the Word of God. Perhaps some of us need to take more private time outside of church to get more accustomed with God.

Look at the standard and the image we label as worship today. I believe we deem worship more as an emotional expression of praise in church and not a dedicated and consistent lifestyle in striving to exhibit the character of God. This "Sunday morning" emotional practice of worship has become so common among people that even though people admit that true worship is supposed to be a daily exemplified display of God's character in their lives, they fail to act on the knowledge.

When we worship God, that is, when we reverence God, He desires us to be sincere. I believe that our sincerity in God's eyes is not perfection by our human perspective but it is rather our consistency in being genuine with God. God wants us to be real in who we are toward Him and toward people. We expect "realness" from God and we want to touch people genuinely, but some of us are barely in touch with who we really are ourselves.

"Those that worship God must worship Him in essence of who they are, and in sincerity." This means if we want to reverence God, we must be real with Him. Why do we continue to come to God with 'spiritual makeup on,' when He knows everything about us before we even gain an understanding about ourselves? We come to the alter all "made-up" and say, "Here I am Lord!" "I'm available!" "My storage is empty!" But before the day is over we are back to feeling like our normal lousy selves. I suppose that it's our emotions that get us mixed up in the moment.

I've discovered that as people, we don't actually have ownership to the ability to pull ourselves out of anything. When God begins to deliver us and cause the essential nature of who we are to rise up to His standard that He has called us, it is a process that God has already started within us. For example, a tree does not grow as we make it. It takes time.

A number of believers have come to a place of artificiality in God. We look good with all our makeup, vintage clothing, educational backgrounds, and fancy job positions and careers, etcetera. However, while according to people, we may be impressive, to God, we still look the same way we did before He allowed us to look impressive. Without God's refinement, we look like the same wretched person we were when He found us.

The problem for some is that they fail to acknowledge that the refinement took place on the inside of them after God started working on them. It doesn't take much to refine a person on the outside: All it takes is working on appearance. However, when a person needs refinement on the inside, it takes more distinct detail and delicacy.

Physically, on the inside of a person, for example, there are a lot of vital "organs" that require careful and stable hands. There are also nerves and arteries that require steady hands to work around. The hands that are working on the inside of us must be thoroughly clean. Some of us need to ask ourselves, who's hands have we allowed to handle us on the inside? Are the hands working on the inside of us, thoroughly clean? Even more so, whose hands are working on us, and is the owner of those hands authorized to handle us?

People of God, we need work on the inside out! What needs the most work in us are our hearts. We need spiritual "heart surgery." Some of us in addition to spiritual "heart surgery" need spiritual brain surgery. Some more of us, need to take our spiritual "prescribed medication" by studying our Bible consistently as we need the strength to endure in our refinement after God's work in us. Our neglect of God's "prescribed medication" (His Word) has caused us to become fragile in the endurance of our faith in God.

There is a way to endure in the faith "in spirit and in truth." The way of enduring in our faith in God is by having the attitude to be of good courage. Having good courage in faith takes consistently moving forward in spite of intimidating discouragement that troubles bring. "Can our worries add a single moment to our lives?" How can it, if we're still here?

Even if our worries come to past, is there still a need to keep worrying? Why do we hold on to worries that have now come to manifestation? Why do we focus on troublesome imaginations that have already taken form? The reality is, if one's worries have come to past, one has to step up and adjust to the situation. Worry is just a thought, reality is a circumstance. "We have to cast down those imaginations."

Imagination exist in the mind, but if it manifest into physical form one can make the choice to either endure in co-existing with it or endure in overcoming it. By nature people fight or flight against worry. When worry becomes an actual situation, we freeze. But we cannot afford to freeze on life because life does not freeze on us. We must learn to adjust. Every soul is able to adjust in time by the grace and power of God.

The only option freezing offers us, is the option of remaining in our circumstance. Freezing in circumstances has the ability to keep the spirit bound because our mind and heart are essentially stuck on what's going on in our lives. "As a man thinks in his heart, so is he." Therefore, if the focus of our heart is stuck on our worries, then essentially our worries are our reality. Essentially, one is dwelling in their imagination.

Do we really want to remain in a life of imagination? Can we live our lives stuck on what could or could not happen? Are we willing to allow unfortunate circumstances to define who we are for the remainder of our lives? The choice is our own!

However, God is always available. Rather we choose to move or not, God is always there. The question is: will we allow God to be glorified by our choice of getting through our circumstances successfully? Can we humble ourselves despite our humbling situations?

It's All Love

I have had a pretty consistent life going to church until my college years. When God started to pull me back into the church, I can't say that I did not recognize the different dynamics of church. For me either church was doing too much or doing too little.

Either or, the church for me, I felt was off track considering the precision of its purpose. To my amazement, in spite of my opinion, I was amazed to see how so many young people were not only attending church faithfully, but were excited to be there; and they were not afraid of expressing their "worship" of God.

I supposed it shocked me when I thought about how differently young people I knew had viewed church when I was going faithfully during high school. Church was not the popular place for a young person to be when I was in high school. I had to become accustomed to this new generation of church, this new era of “church with attitude”.

The more I continued to attend, the more my young peers challenged me because I felt like I was now the odd man out. Now isn't that something? When I attended church faithfully during high school, I was the odd man out. Now even still at this point, here I am post college attending church again, and I'm still the odd man out.

I used to feel like I was looked at as spiritually ignorant when I would attend Bible Study. No one would say anything, but when I would give my input during an open discussion at Bible Study, based upon what I knew about God personally, you would have thought I was speaking in tongues considering how awkward it felt. However, I continued to go to church and started to study my Bible more, and I haven't stopped since.

The fact that I felt I was being viewed as spiritually incompetent in my knowledge of who God was spiritually challenged me to know God all the more. I knew that I knew God because my mother always taught my sister and I about God. By the same token, I've seen God work so miraculously within my family, and more specifically in my household, helping my Mom to raise me, my sister, and my nephew.

So I studied, and I prayed, and I fasted, and unexpectedly the craziest thing started to happen. In actuality, it's not so crazy now, but back then it was hard to understand. It seemed the closer I got to God the more people close in my life started to become more and more distant from me.

I fell in love with God so the hardest part was allowing people that I knew in my life to become distant and even let some connections and relationships die. However, we never really lose in God. Things are more-so refined so we get a different perspective. It's necessary for the ordained purpose God is bringing us to.

Some of us have God in the wrong position. Therefore, when we respond to God's call to get things in order, as He prepares us in our purpose for Him, our perception and the perception of others involved in the change of reposition, feel the shift. That feeling of the shift is a spiritual feeling where they must disconnect from us. Some people reconnect to us in a new position, as God reassembles us in refinement. Other people remain disconnected from us, as God's reassembling of us does not have room for some folk we were once connected to.

This is because when God's Word has taken root in us its effect on us is extremely potent. It's so potent that it causes a spiritual reaction that some people won't be able to handle while God is working in us. Some people will no longer be able to handle us at all. When the Word of God settles in our hearts- the core of our belief, it purges us from the inside out. This purge is like a fragrance that is so strong that some people need to exit the room for a while before finally being able to get accustomed to it; others just leave entirely.

The reality is, when God gets a handle on us, there are some people in our lives who once had a hand in our lives but now must take their hands off of us. We become untouchable spiritually, because when God's hands are on us, and He is at work with us for His purpose and our benefit, God won't risk anyone, not even our own selves, to soil His workmanship. We are the workmanship of God, and we are forged in His love. God's love will sometimes hurt when the time comes for us to be purged, so we can produce what He desires out of our lives.

When God's hands are on us people will find it hard to handle us. Once again, we become untouchable, spiritually. People find it hard to get a grip on us because God's hands are covering us. How can anyone seize what is already besieged? How can anyone possess what God has in His possession? God's hands are too big and too strong for anyone to come and take us out of them once He has “cupped” us in His purpose. The reason people can't handle the new life we find in God is because we're now in His hands.

In God's hands there is love. This is a different kind of love. It is a love so great that there is "no greater love" than this love. This love has a name, and the name of this love is

Jesus Christ, who is also God, and God is love. God is real love, and real love loves too much to allow us to fall out of love.

Therefore, in order for people who are corrupt by fear, to stay in love with Love, God who is love, has to hurt us sometimes. God has to purge us, over and over again, so we can stay in Him; so that we can stay in Love. Therefore, we must have failures. We must have heartaches. We must have disappointments. We must experience deaths. These things are going to keep us connected to God and thereby keep us in Love: Here is the problem in the church. Here is the problem with the church.

The problem is the church has fallen out of love with God. We've fallen out of love with Love Himself. Like all relationships gone bad, we have become so focused on trying to find out how to please God that we fail to seek Him out in regard to what actually pleases Him. Like all relationships gone bad, we have ruined the relationship with God. We are experiencing a breakup with Him because of our neglect of minding the little things, because we've been too busy focusing on the big things.

We know the big things in the church today: Vision is a big thing. "Kingdom living" is a big thing. Finances are a big thing. "Shouting" is a big thing. Promise is a big thing. Ministry is a big thing. Now while there isn't anything wrong with these "big things," the problem is that these big things are so big that we lose focus on the "little things" that actually are what matters.

The little things appear minor to us but they are major to God. We can tell who really knows God based on them knowing better than to focus on the "big things" over the "little things". The little things are love, obedience, consistency, actual holiness (not the strive to holiness), and faith. These things are so little we can't even hope to touch them physically, but spiritually they are too big for the world to grasp.

While they are intangible things physically, they are tangible spiritually. Their potency is what really makes the world go round; and they have the power to turn society inside out. They are so powerful to grasp now because they each challenge the ways of the world we live in today. Love, obedience, consistency, holiness, and faith, but especially love, are the real weapons of mass destruction, and they are foreign objects in modern humanity.

So where is the love? Why is it off? Well, to begin, the world at large does not recognize love because the world isn't looking for love. True love is found in the Holy Spirit, as a gift after receiving Jesus Christ. As the world rejects Jesus, in all he is, they miss the gift by default. They miss the gift of the Holy Spirit by rejecting Jesus, which in turn, they reject God; thereby rejecting the very identity of love in essence.

Love can only be received in order to give it. We don't give away love "so to speak," but we share love. We share love by remaining in Christ. We remain in Christ by internalizing the Word of God as we study the Bible. By this we learn God, we learn how to die to ourselves, and we learn how to mirror Jesus Christ.

This reflects on our character, as it sinks and settles into our integrity. As a result, we start to mirror Christ in our lives, and by this, we exemplify the image and likeness of God through the exemplified integrity of character of Jesus Christ.

It sounds simple, but people fail to do this because they don't believe. People don't believe in Jesus fully in this world, and even the church, because they either have chosen not to believe in Christ, or they are blind to Christ because they don't know the Word intimately. It is not about how many scriptures we are distinctively knowledgeable about; God can care less about that. It is about what we know intimately based on the Holy Spirit teaching us to comprehend the Word as a result of the Holy Spirit giving us understanding.

We fail to love because we fail to know the Word of God intimately. Therefore, we don't know Jesus Christ intimately, which means we don't know God intimately either. "He who has an ear let him hear." Hear in this case means to listen and understand. There is a process to comprehending the Word so that we can receive love.

First, we have to have an ear for the Word, which means we have to give it our essential and sincere attention. Second, we have to listen to the Word, and we do this by our action of being essentially sincere in our will to acknowledge the Word attentively. Third, we have to come to understand the Word, and we do this by comprehending what the Word says so we can live by the Word.

We must give attention to the Word, be attentive to the Word, and gain comprehension to the Word. One can't live by the Word if one doesn't understand the Word. One can't understand the Word if one does not have a will to learn it. God gives us this will to want to come to know Him.

Learning the Word is a form of worship because it is a form of giving reverence to God. Don't forget "those who worship God must worship Him in spirit, and in truth." The flip side to this being, "those who worship God must worship Him, in the essence of who they are, and in sincerity of who they are".

Therefore, if I am a liar, it's best for me to come before God humble, in the honesty that I am a liar. If I am a fornicator, it's best to come before God humble, in the honesty that I am a fornicator. If I am homosexual, it's best to come before God humble, in the honesty that I am a homosexual. If I am a murderer, it's best to come before God, humble, in the honesty that I am a murderer.

Coming before God humble and in the honesty of who we are is key when it comes to reverence. Worship is reverence. Reverencing without repentance, where repentance is required, is the quickest way to get cut off before a King, not to mention a Sovereign God.

There are liars in the church. There are fornicators in the church. There are even murderers in the church. There are also definitely homosexuals in the church. This is also true if this is who one is at heart and not by action. How many of us are guilty at heart, although void of the action?

However, this being who we are essentially and sincerely is not the biggest issue? Christ came for those who know they are these things, and agree that being these things are wrong. The problem in the church is that we deliver ourselves to God as such, but we fail to repent for who we are.

We get saved by saying "I believe", but no spiritual surgery takes place. For example, we stop the action of homosexuality but we linger in the ideal homosexuality. So there is delivery but no deliverance! Whenever there is delivery and no deliverance, the corrupt nature of who we were remains on the inside and it spoils the love in us that we received. Don't let the love you receive spoil the love you can become.

I believe the lack of love is one of the biggest issues in the church. We fail in Love because our love is out of place. In all the mess we are, we cannot love another based on love for ourselves alone. Why? Because a good number of us don't love ourselves. Jesus Christ taught us how to position our love and in what position we are to love. In fact, these commands are the greatest commandments God has given us so that we can love correctly, and this love is love by God's own standards.

According to Christ, first, "We are to love The Lord, our God, with all our heart, all our mind, all our soul, and all our strength." Second in order, but yet equal to this first commandment, "We are to love our neighbor as ourselves." Here is the issue! There are many people in the world, and many people in the church, who do not love themselves. I pose to us, that we do not truly love ourselves because we don't truly love God first.

We don't love God first because we haven't put Him first. Further, we don't love God because we don't know Him intimately through His Word. Therefore, we don't love correctly because we don't know who Jesus Christ is intimately, as a result of not knowing the Word (the Bible) intimately.

Christ also gave us a new commandment. He said, "We are to love one another. Just as HE loved us, so are we to love one another." If we don't come to know the Word of God intimately, as a result of giving our attention to the Word, by listening to the Word attentively, and understanding the Word by comprehending it, we won't know the love of Jesus Christ.

Once we come to know the love of Jesus Christ, we will see how much God loves us. By this we fall in love with God (if we're His), and we come to love ourselves as we come to identify ourselves as a part of God. As we learn this love for ourselves, based on God's love for us, shown and exemplified through His Word, we can love others with the same love that we received from God. As a result, it's all Love- this being it's all God, and God alone is good, then we can truly say, "It's all good!"

We, the church, have failed in loving one another. Due to our failure and unwillingness to love one another, the world that looks to us, is losing faith in God. They lose faith in God and therefore reject Jesus Christ. Therefore, they miss the gift which is the Holy Spirit, and they never receive Love. We have to rekindle our love for Love- God, and show the world what Love (God) looks like.

We cannot do this without knowing Jesus Christ intimately. We cannot know Christ intimately if we don't "study the Word to be approved unto God," pray, and fast to be obedient. When we fail to do these things, failing in building and maintaining our personal relationship with God, we fail God, by being disobedient in our misrepresentation of whom we are supposed to be. Perhaps we are not who we think we are.

~ Chapter Ten ~

I KNOW I'M SOMEBODY

Accepting Abnormal Me

I am imperfect! In fact, the only thing perfect in society is the imperfections of people. None of us are void of fault, adversity, infirmity, and trial. This is what makes a man a person. By accepting that we are imperfect is how we can find dependency in Jesus Christ and appreciate the transparency of the Word.

Indeed, we are all born subject to adversity. However, I have found being born to adversity to be beneficial. Being born to adversity authenticates our blessed assurance. After adversity shakes our found affirmation in who we think we are in Christ, God will always assure us toward true refined confidence in Him, to complete what he purposed us to do.

For example, the Apostle, Simon Peter, denied Christ three times before Christ died, but after Christ rose, He reassured Peter that he actually did love him and was worthy of him (John 21).

Before we are perfected in God, we must be proven in the fires of our adversity. This proves to us our worth in Christ. God has no need of proving to Himself the potential of what He created: He already knows. God wants us to be assured that we are His chosen, based on who He purposed us to be in spite of who we are. We all need work regarding who we are, but in the end, the only thing that matters is the fact that we belong to God.

Many of us question who we are in Christ, and the potential we have in him. We do this based on our own definition of who we are, which is almost always based upon the reality of the persons, places, and things we are connected to. Once again, our corrupt human instinct to define ourselves causes us to confuse our potential and purpose.

It is alright to question ourselves. This is inevitable not to do as a human being. However, we question ourselves using the wrong questions. We shouldn't question if we have the potential to be the person that Christ chose to fulfill the purpose that we know intimately is meant for us. The answer is proven to us in our will to strive to continue in Christ. The Word of God is the key to unlocking our potential toward fulfilling our purpose in God.

So often today, we get wrapped up in who we are, and God has to allow adversity to challenge our ego. When this happens will we continue to press forward amid adversity? This is the challenge God uses to bring us to a blessed assurance. This is an assurance that refines our perspective of who we are and helps us to acknowledge and accept the truth about us entirely. The truth being- we are called despite the positives and negatives of who we are.

The perfect thing about being imperfect is that imperfect people can relate to other imperfect people. This is the perfection of unity among men- "one nation under God, indivisible, with liberty and justice for all." How can we be one, if we can't relate? How can we be one in liberty if we are separated in the shame of our imperfections? How can we unite to a place of justice for all if we are hiding the nasty truths about us behind barriers of falsehood?

The barriers that hide our true selves already cause us to be separated. The fact that this country and people around the world hide their flaws is why we find it so difficult to relate to one another. No one wants to be big enough to speak the truth and say, "I'm hurt!" or "This bothers me!" or "I'm weak in this area!"

People in society are so scared of difference. We're so afraid to stand up strong despite the fact that our strength has been decreasing for so long. It takes a strong person to stand up in shame to overcome more blows, after already taking powerful blows to sensitive areas. Where is the endurance of the people?

I have learned that with endurance comes patience and with patience comes wisdom. Sometimes we have to endure sticks and stones long enough to know how to block them so we can overcome them toward our destination. So many good people go bad because instead of overcoming their troubles, they override their troubles.

An override is nothing but a jump to progression. Overcoming on the other hand, is a triumph of grace that is worthy of gratification by way of endurance. The strength to endure comes through Christ (Philippians 4:13).

As long as we live, we are going to need grace in our lives. In fact, we can't get through life alive without grace granted to us through mercy. People all over the world have seen dreams come true and gained prosperous lives because someone took a chance on them anyway by simply showing mercy. I dare to ask, what man is a man without the residue of mercy in their lives? Somewhere in our time on Earth, we ought to have a moment where someone showed us mercy, and in vice versa.

We are becoming cold in our nature. We now reject mercy because we think it shows we're weak. We reject grace because we think it shows we're vulnerable. We reject miracles because we think it shows that we are not as good, smart, certified, or perfect, as we like to seem. Is there any person in the world that is still truthful in the fact that they are only human and therefore, imperfect?

Accepting abnormal me is all about accepting the truth that we are human. The problem is we are trying to be perfect people, or we either accept that perfection is not a goal worthy of attempting so we live life the way we see fit. It is time for society to wake up and become human again.

"We are to be perfect as God is perfect," not as mankind is perfect. Mankind is not, and will never be perfect without God's Word. It is the human spirit-that being, the spirit of a person, that we are to perfect. We fail because we remain in our effort chasing perfection in our temporary lives and not our preparation for eternal life through following the way, the truth, and the life which is Jesus Christ.

Qualifying Quality

Every morning before my sister and I would depart from my mother to go to school, she would always have us say, "I know I'm somebody, cause God don't make no junk." My Mom had my sister and I say this ever since we were in pre-school. Mom had good reason for why she would always have us say this. While it may sound very programming and old fashion, it was ingeniously fun.

Mom would say, "I know I'm somebody, why y'all?" Smiling and laughing, Shira and I would yell back, enthusiastically, "Cause God don't make no junk!" Smiling back, laughing, Mom would say, "Yeaess".

Like most parents in my neighborhood, Mom didn't make much money. My sister and I were down to one adult in our home. However, Mom, to this day, was strong. I have never seen her cry until my senior year of high school and my freshman year of college. She is one that is not afraid to show anyone her relationship with God. Although, Mom has not been perfect all the time, as she's human, she is perfect in how she has always "acknowledged God in all her ways." Things always worked out someway somehow, we always progressed forward.

Mom was far from rich financially, but she is wealthy in God's grace and mercy. Her bank account was in Jesus Christ, who she calls, the equalizer. The integrity she has in God, through her intimate knowledge of Jesus was undeniable; and she passed her wealth of knowledge of Christ to my sister and I. Mom gave us everything because she gave us all she knew about Jesus. Sometimes our knowledge of God is all we have to give. But there is nothing greater to give than the knowledge of God by way of Jesus Christ.

Mom taught my sister and me the importance of having a personal relationship with God, and I internalized it. Crazy thing was, I didn't start grasping what Mom taught me until recently. However, I've made some significant progress when I look over my life. God has truly blessed me to continue on forward. Through it all, I've learned that the greatest strength of some of us, is not our level of knowledge, neither our skill of strength, not even our passion of heart. For some of us, our greatest strength to progress forward in life is our integrity of character in Christ.

You have to know who you are by a different angle and a different perspective. You have to know who you belong to, and more importantly, you have to know through whom you have being. A lot of people don't know who they are, because they don't acknowledge God, or they don't believe in Jesus Christ.

"It is in God that we live, move, and have our being." Through Christ we and everything known to mankind was made. Jesus Christ is the essential source of everything essentially. It is Christ who truly qualifies the quality of a person.

Human beings are like machines. Like a battery that gives a machine life, we have a built-in source of life, that is an essential part of us, and it needs to be charged often from time to time. Every built-in battery needs a charger that connects it to the source of power that keeps it alive. Our battery is our spirit. Our charger is the Holy Spirit. Our source of power is Jesus Christ who connects into the main source of power-God the Father.

To remain in the good quality of who we are, all we have to do is stay connected to Jesus Christ. I must say, from what I see in regard to African Americans, we have not stayed connected to Christ. This disconnection to Christ shows up in the lifestyle of many Africans Americans today. We are running low on power, and I dare to even say, we are currently in the "red zone"- the critical percentage of life.

We become fancy by connecting to portable sources that may work well but are limited in themselves. How can anything not connected to a main source maintain what's connected to it? They are both portable, and both of them will eventually "burn out."

This is the condition of not only African Americans living without Christ, but any group of people who live without Christ. People without Christ are somewhat like portable tangible objects. We allow ourselves to be dependent on other objects that are also tangibly portable.

This puts us at risk to die because we've allowed ourselves to depend on an object that has equal or less quality to sustain and satisfy us. We are foolish to depend on this object of equal or less quality, as we base the quality of the object on the quantity of life sustenance and satisfaction that the object presents to us. It's foolish because we fail to acknowledge that the object we are depending on is no more valuable and no more powerful than we are.

By the same token, we fail to see that some objects are less valuable and less fragile than we are. Sadly, we still depend on objects that are worth less or weaker than we are, and we rely on them for sustenance and satisfaction with our lives, only to become slaves to these people, places, and things, by default. This happens often in society today. It happens because we misjudge quality by our steady focus of quantity.

Due to our misjudgment of what quality is, we put value on a person, place, or thing we can count on. Today's society doesn't count what it is not able to calculate.

I guess we could say that it takes faith to have faith. The reason we lack in faith is because we lack in the quality of faith. We lack in the quality of faith because we lack in the quality of true love. True love comes from God through Jesus Christ. Christ gives us the gift of true love through the truth we gain from the Holy Spirit.

Not Bound to the Block

The hood is only a mentality, and the mentality is hood! That means, the way we think as a community of people as a whole, is the way our community is perceived. The way we perceive and then act in our own communities will in turn cause others to make their own assumptions of our communities based upon our behavior.

If the mentality of the people in our communities is a "hood" mentality, then the behavior of our communities will generally shape our communities as a "hood". The way we are in essence reflects who we are essentially. If we perceive ourselves in a particular way, then how we perceive ourselves is what we will be. Many of us behave the way we do in the hood not because we have no choice, but in actuality, it is because we continue to choose that this will be the way we will be.

Without a doubt, this choice is birthed from fear, anger, and frustration. However, corruptors of this sort must never dictate to a person who they must be. We are still enslaved, now in our minds. We must choose our freedom, and true freedom only comes from the source of who we are.

Wherever we come from or start from naturally does not speak for who we are. God speaks, and has already spoken for who we are. This is a truthful fact for everyone and everything everywhere.

Nothing, no one, and nowhere, can lay claim to our destiny, and who we are essentially. Nothing, no one, and nowhere, can label who we really are, our choice of integrity, or the essential purpose God has for us. Ultimately, nothing, no one, and nowhere, can label what God already has claim to, through us belonging to Jesus Christ.

Living the hood life or living the hard life is viewed as the reality for some. Some people live the life they live because they sincerely don't know any better or any different. How people are raised in the type of families we are born into play a major role in how we turn out to be.

People are programmed into being who they come to be, not just artificially but naturally. We are indeed human beings and not machines, but we are prone to being programmed. Major factors that influence how we are "programmed" include who raises us, the environment we're raised in, our beliefs, and simply how we naturally are. How we simply are naturally determines what we can and cannot tolerate in life.

Part of living the human experience is gaining the understanding that we are constantly being "programmed" and "deprogrammed" daily as we live. In our daily lives, what we learn and experience increases and decreases our perception of life. This is why studying our Bible, praying, fasting, and exercising our faith by living out the Word of God is important.

All these things we do is feeding our spirit a healthy and balanced spiritual meal. Feeding ourselves spiritually from a balanced and healthy manor, as aligned with Christ, is what keeps us nourished. This allows us to accept what's good for our spirit and reject what's bad for our spirit automatically. This is similar to how our own bodies reject what's bad for us and accepts what's good for us.

The interesting part of all this is that sometimes we really don't know for sure what's good or what's bad for our bodies until we see from experience. However, because our spirit is the essential part of who we are, God loves us enough to give us His Word to teach us how to nourish our spirit to satisfaction and sustainability.

In all our ways, it is essential that we acknowledge Christ, and God's spirit will direct us. Some of us need direction to get to where we are going. We are tired of where we're at, and we're frustrated with trying to figure out how to get there. This is a tough situation to be in, but we can get to where we're supposed to be. All we have to do is forsake what we think we know about our beginning and get into the beginning of how we came into being.

How we came into being and where we started is not in poverty. It is not in violence. It is not in oppression or hopelessness, not even slavery, or the glory of being the potential original race. The source of where we came into being, and how we came into being, is in glory in Christ. Therefore, we must return to glory so that we can find glorification in our lives.

We return to glory not to seize glory but to bask in glory. Jesus Christ is where we started. "Christ is the author of our lives." We must bask in the glory of Christ, as he is the source of who we are, and how everything came into being.

Satisfaction and sustenance are not factors that can be chased. We are either satisfied or we're not. We are either sustained or we're not. Satisfaction and sustenance are meant to be seized. We seize satisfaction and sustenance by basking in them. They are found in Jesus Christ.

Therefore, when we come to the realization where we want to be bound to Christ because we cannot be sustained or satisfied by basking in the necessities of the "block", we will find fulfillment in who we are and everything associated with the truth of who we are. This truth isn't found in who we are but rather in where we essentially came. We came from Jesus Christ. "In Christ we live, move, and have our being." It is in Jesus Christ that we essentially exist. Amen!

Bearers of Glory

People have a tendency to blame Satan for all their faults and wicked ways. I've learned that sin nature has caused human nature to become corrupt in its essence. "In this flesh dwells no good thing." As I mentioned before, not only do people want to be godly, we want to be God.

It's interesting to me that even in our effort to be godlike, claiming to live for God, we all (to some measurable degree) have an itch to take God's place. So many people by human nature want to be God by identity and not just integrity. This is probably because we can be so blind and bound to the character trait of human image.

Satan introduced us to the error that caused him to fall, and deceived us into falling the same way. As a result, we inherited his attributes of wicked desire and his corrupt nature. By nature we are left corrupt, deceived out of the glorified beings we once were by original design.

Seeking salvation we hunger for satisfaction. All the while seeking satisfaction in one another, we desire the scraps of mortal sustenance. This is not enough to ease our hunger that can only be soothed by consuming Jesus Christ. Christ is the bread of life- the true bread of Heaven, the spiritual food that nourishes our hunger and causes us to grow in glory.

Growing in glory is a process and can only be obtained through seeking Christ. As we seek Christ we seek the retribution that we desire for ourselves. Yet I've found this retribution to be retribution against our own nature. We are bearers of glory defiled of glory.

When the spirit is nourished by its source it gains strength, and once it finds its strength, the spirit will fight. Christ didn't come for peace but to set the world on fire with truth. This fire purges even us, and the purging comes from the Holy Spirit. The Holy Spirit brings conviction, and with conviction comes correction.

Our human nature does not like correction when it is inflicted. It's human nature to reject anything that it does not agree with. However, it is the spirits nature to also reject what it does not agree with. What the spirit does not agree with is our human nature.

As long as we remain in our human nature we will never find restoration in the former glory we originated from. Once again this is why we remain in an unsatisfied state, constantly searching for satisfaction after satisfaction. We look for satisfaction in bits and pieces.

Finding glorification in satisfaction is a process that may come in bits and pieces in our pursuit of it, but the glory of satisfaction is whole. True satisfaction, true glory, is not a fraction, it is wholeness. Imagine how whole we can be when basking in the essence of the source of all that we are. This is true glorification.

Without Christ, mankind has lost their glory. Further, we are deceived of glory and we rob ourselves of the satisfaction of glorification when we seek it in ourselves. If we could find satisfaction in ourselves why would we seek satisfaction?

I believe in this life one cannot find total satisfaction. It is human nature that keeps us from fulfilling fulfillment. There is always something that we are moving forward to in order to survive or find comfort. God blesses us by sustaining us, allowing all our needs to be supplied as we are needy beings. We are needy by nature because our human nature is "naughty by nature."

Therefore Jesus Christ, the source of who we are, sent us the Holy Spirit. The Holy Spirit fills the voids that we have spiritually, and comforts us in these voids. We cannot have true comfort without the presence of God. God has not yet left this Earth void of His presence.

Even when the Earth ignores God's presence, He has always left someone who carries His presence to comfort the world. Today, with the gift of the Holy Spirit, those who are in Christ are the bearers of God's presence. That's why we have to mind our actions, so that we don't defile the host we carry. The host we carry is God's Spirit. How many of us know what we're carrying and the potency of what we carry?

This is why some people are nasty to us for no reason: As we carry the Holy Spirit we challenge people by our very presence. Things can't just be normal when those who carry God's Spirit are around. Those who carry the Holy Spirit cause people to be exposed. Therefore folk get defensive, they get touchy.

People become irritated and uncomfortable. Why? Because when we carry the Holy Spirit we carry the "Spirit of truth," and truth will always disclose or bring closure. Carriers of the Holy Spirit, you bring out the essential truth of a person. Our essence brings a sense of satisfaction in spite of lack because of the potent spiritual fragrance that God's Spirit essentially gives off.

We need God's presence in order to have supernatural peace, joy, and happiness. They are supernatural because when we naturally lack peace, joy, and happiness, we are still in need of these three attributes to get us through life, and survive.

I believe people who kill themselves, even when they have everything, do so because they lack supernatural peace, supernatural joy, and supernatural happiness. We need to have peace, joy, and happiness supernaturally, because anything that is "supernatural" has an essential nature. In other words, anything supernatural cannot be made from any combining factors in any natural or tangibly needed amount. It just exists in all purity that cannot be subtracted from or added to- it is pure in nature.

Mankind is no longer pure in the nature of our being. However, we still obtain a spirit, and because we obtain a spirit a portion of us exist in supernatural essence. Therefore, we can obtain attributes of supernatural essence, but we can only obtain them with the gift that comes from the source of all we are- Jesus Christ. The gift in a sense is handed down from source to direct resource of the source.

Our spirits are direct resources of the source- the source being Jesus Christ, God's Son. We are the direct resources of Jesus Christ because we and everything known in this world was made through him. Jesus Christ is the direct resource of God the Father.

As Christ remains in God, he is one with Him, and God sends the Holy Spirit to us as a gift we acquire after receiving Jesus. When we acquire the Holy Spirit we connect directly to God who is the source of Jesus Christ. We bask in the glory of God by essentially denying ourselves and allowing Him to have all the glory over our lives.

MORE (My Ordained Right to be Effective)

This life is temporary, and we should not bind ourselves to this life, but this life is precious. We will never again see the beauty of the corruption we are now. I reckon that God wants us to value both lives by glorifying Him before we return to Him dressed in the glory of eternity and immortality.

What is a man, but a memory landscaped in time by God- the architect of our soul? We are nothing but shadows and dust, and we return to the same. I pose to us all that death is in the order and decency of mortal life.

I am young, and in my young life I have held to the wisdom of cherishing this life. Why not cherish it? God grants us the gift of life in two shades. One life is silver, the other life is gold. Yet they are both treasures that God has graced us and gifted us to have.

I never knew why, but it upsets my soul how much mankind under-values life. We abuse our mortality by claiming it our own; and we forsake our immortality by neglecting the author of life himself- Jesus Christ. Today, people fail to understand just how precious we are in totality.

We are more than what we esteem ourselves to be. We are more by essential definition. As we realize the "more" that we are essentially, we experience refinement. This experience of refinement is a sense of affirmation: affirming who God has made us to be, and not we our-selves.

We are more, as it is our right to be as children of God. I always desired to be more. In my ignorance of God, I've chased it, before I discovered that in actuality, "more" was essentially who I was. I am more because I am a child of God: it is My Ordained Right to be Effective- MORE.

As children of God we have an ordained right to be effective in this world. As Christians, we are no more of this world then Jesus is. However, although we are not of this world does not mean we're not in it. We exist in this world, and it is not our duty to conform to it but it is our duty to confound it.

I and likely others, have questioned what it is that we can give and leave a world that we don't belong to and rejects us? I've found the answer is to just acknowledge and follow God at all times. In every aspect of our lives we must include God, and allow Him to lead, even past our will. We have to learn to fight our will and allow God's will to consume us.

That's a hard thing to do, but there is peace, happiness, and joy in doing so.

We have to just be; allowing our very lives to be the light we wish to show the world to the glory of God. Our light shines by living in truth, and living in the truth of who we are. As we live in Christ, we live in the truth by obeying and depending on God's Word. I know intimately that I don't need to question "if this nation's foundation ever lived in total truth".

A partial truth is not the truth at all. Truth doesn't keep one guessing. Truth assures us in what we are seeking. Truth reproves us to approval and proof.

For centuries, this nation has spoken out in partial truth, but we never seemed to speak out in all truth. To this very day, American society fails to get to the core root of our nations issues. We fail to state the simple stuff- bringing light to our nasty faces. By habit, we've developed a lifestyle that covers up the truth, because the truth about truth is that truth can get nasty. However, truth itself isn't nasty, but what truth exposes is what is nasty.

We fail to realize the "more" that exist in us because we spend too much time trying to cover it up. We subtract from the truth of our lives, instead of counting this progress in victorious addition to our lives. We use degrees, money, titles, careers, etcetera to extinguish the light of who we really are. That light could simply be, a simple skinny black boy from South Philly who can't identify any strong successful talents other than his voiced thoughts. That's truth!

We look at the truth about ourselves as such, and frown upon it and say this isn't going to be me. Yet, on the contrary, it is exactly who we are. It's a bad habit and a sad reality of oneself to reject the truth about one's self. Everyone has their place that they must start in life.

Although our place at the starting line may appear to be behind everyone else, this does not mean that we're at a disadvantage. It's all about how we view our place at the starting line that determines our attitude in the race. Our attitude in the race is a reflection of our mentality.

The reflection of our mentality exposes us spiritually. People can sense insecurity, as insecurity is one of mankind's biggest common imperfections. We can all relate to insecurity in some way, form, or fashion; but insecurity is still a part of the truth of who and what we are. Why would we chase perfection, security, and satisfaction in any form if we were truly whole within ourselves?

Seeing ourselves for who we really are is a process of refinement which consists of rebuilding from the inside out. Refinement from the inside reflects its results on the outside. This is not just in the sense of the appearance of the person, but also where the person will choose to appear.

A person who is truly new needs new scenery. New scenery brings with it new exposure. New exposure brings about new experiences. New experiences bring new encounters. New encounters awake new awareness. New awareness has the potential to grow and change who we are into a new person.

As we continue to live, we are able to see that we are more than what meets the eye. If there was ever a definition that we could use to define mankind, it would simply be "more". Moving forward, mankind will keep changing in who we are and what we are capable of. This is good and bad news regarding the potential of how man will view them-selves in the future.

Better found Dumbfounded

I think that the greatest strength and weakness of people has been our intelligence. Time and time again, people have proven unable to handle ingenious. Our wit makes us arrogant and therefore "pridefully" ignorant. While one would think our intelligence brings us security, the arrogance in our intelligence proves we are insecure by the prideful ignorance we show by being arrogant.

People have become so arrogant in the limitless findings of the human mind that we use to challenge God. Worse, we even twist the Bible to benefit ourselves, ignorant to the fact that the Bible is meant to benefit us by keeping us in order due to our corrupt human nature. The nature of man is liable to the nature of sin. Therefore, it is only natural that we have laws to keep us liable that have been written by God. Laws that are not written by man are essentially not subject to the corrupt nature of humanity. If they were they wouldn't need to be changed so much.

No matter how hard we try not to, it is human nature to desire rule or authority over the Earth and one another. We were created to have dominion over the Earth. It's in our nature to do so. The problem is that as we have been perverted by sin, our natural desire to have dominion over the Earth has also become distorted. There is always more than one way to do things, but there is always one right way to do things: that is the sole way- the correct way of doing something.

People were given dominion over the Earth not over one another. Our method of stewardship is where we fail in the world and in the church. Our method of stewardship is why people lack. Sin is what perverts stewardship because it corrupts love. One cannot know true stewardship without knowing true love. True love is selfless and it is true, never biased or confusing, and it never contradicts itself in selfishness.

We've lost sight of stewardship and love when we took our eyes off God and placed our focus in ourselves. We are self-aware by nature but when we become self-centered in who we are, we forsake the reality that we are nothing without our Maker. Jesus Christ is our maker, and we've become so numb to our own intelligence that we have outsmarted ourselves into a false belief in Jesus' full identity.

I've noticed how people speak of Jesus Christ, and it is cruel, disrespectful, and very arrogant. After all these years since Christ dwelt among us, in the flesh, we still mock him. Further, we attack him by attacking the belief and standards of his followers. However, understand that no one attacks what they don't believe.

How can we attack something that we don't see? The truth is we really do see the truth. Many of us are scared to put faith in what we must have faith in. This would require accepting years of us being false with others and ourselves. Accepting the truth and moving forward despite any falsehoods we've been living in is a "walking on water" experience.

Nobody likes "walking on water," because in order to do that, one has to first get out the boat. The boat would be our comfort zone- what makes sense: what we can understand and comprehend. The boat is what we can compute: the nature of how we, as human beings, think. The boat is the essence of our mentality as human beings.

There is control in the boat. We can navigate at our own will in the boat; but what happens when the circumstances surrounding our boat compromises our reliance of the boat? What happens when the way we think is not enough to change our situation?

I think at some point in life, everyone arrives at a place where we can't think our way out of a situation. In fact, we arrive at situations that are impossible to do and accept logically. As a African American male in this country, I and I'm sure other black males, can relate when I say that sometimes, and maybe even all the time, logic is a comfort that we wish could solve all our problems. Yet logic for the average black man can often seem circumstantially insane or situationally incomputable.

A major part of the struggle for African Americans, especially black males, is getting things to add up. Furthermore, hoping for things to work out despite it being logically clear that what we are hoping for looks impossible. This is where God comes in, which requires us to get out the boat of our comfortable mentality, and "walk on water."

Sometimes the only thing we can count on knowing for sure is the reality that we are in a real situation where we have no control. When this happens all we can do is focus and depend on Jesus to keep our feet solid on nothing solid. That's actually where I'm at now: A place where I can only just be- a place of no definition.

It's a challenge to just be. How can a human being, who's very nature is to define every aspect of their life, just be? How can we live in vacancy of purpose, understanding, and reason?

I've found my comfort of this question in another question? - Who are we to define who we are and where we're at in life? Some of us are able to define every aspect of our lives, and sadly in God's eyes we are vacant. Some people are living well but living amiss because they have chosen to live life to the fullest, as they see fit, according to their own standards and will.

Our ingenious has brought us to an era in society where we no longer feel a need for God, and we further denounce the relevance of Jesus Christ. However, without Christ we are nothing but renegade souls, and this is what many have become. This is because we have "leaned to our own understanding". By this, we have come to settlement in perverse logic and reason which has led us to reject our fear (sense of reverence) of God.

If we're not with Christ we're against him. If we are void of Christ we are potentially against him because we allow ourselves to be open to be perverted. When we accept Christ sincerely, we align ourselves in him and receive the Holy Spirit. It is the Holy Spirit that then becomes our logic and our reason.

As society rejects Christ, it automatically neglects the Holy Spirit that is freely available from God. A society that lacks the Holy Spirit lacks the consciousness of God. It is the conscience of God that allows us to have wisdom, and with His wisdom, we have the ability to judge and discern righteously based on the knowledge of God Himself. It is God's consciousness that convicts us and not our own reason. Without the Holy Spirit people reason wrong into right. Selah!

~ Chapter Eleven ~

WALKING ON WATER

Everybody Ain't You!

Whenever I felt I was cheated or treated unfairly for no reason, I often would get very upset, questioning why. In response, my mom always said (as only she could say), "Everybody ain't you, Shalom!" I used to get so mad whenever she said it, but as I grew in Christ, I found myself accepting this more easily.

We are all unique, and we are all one of a kind. God has taken his time to make each of us, and He knows each of us by name. Growing up, and even sometimes now, I struggled with getting treated fairly. People always seemed to mishandle or misuse me. This infuriated me because I always tried to do the right thing, even in "doing me".

I think it's better for us to be misused than mishandled, because if we're mishandled we are at risk of becoming broken. In opposition to this, by being misused, at least we're handled properly, just too much or too little. To simplify being misused, there are people who use us the wrong way, but when they're done, although we maybe burned out passed the limit, we‘re not broken. However, there are some people who handle us the wrong way all together, without regard for our well-being, and we end up fractured or broken. This may cause us to never be the same again.

People can be extremely rough, cruel, and inhumane. In my young life, I've learned that hard people harden people. "Iron sharpens iron." No matter what the iron is being sharpened for, this truth still stands. People who once had cutting edge potential by being sharpened by what was compatible, have been made rugged because they were beat on by what was not necessary.

This happens when we allow ourselves to be unequally yoked by people, places, and things. The life and the lifestyle that God has prescribed for you can be totally different for somebody else, even if the destination or the outcome is the same. God has made each of us unique and has given us our own life, and our own path back to glory in Him.

Although there is one direction to God, through Jesus Christ alone, the routes are personal. Society is becoming rough and bitter because we are taking the same "routes" as others. Don't take anyone's word for the Word, not even your own, get the Word from God yourself.

Many of us will never be satisfied with who we are because we won't put aside our consideration for others opinions of who we are. More critically, many more will never be satisfied in life and reach higher potential because we stand on the Word (the Bible) based on other people's interpretations alone. How many people are miserable and Hell bound because they won't come to know God for themselves?

The sad thing about this is if we never knew God, can we say that we really ever knew ourselves? We are nothing without God, and in order to truly know who God is, we must come to know who Jesus is. If we don't know Christ for ourselves, we actually don't know all that we are. All that we are is found in Christ. Christ is the origin, story, and legacy of who we are in truth.

We have to be truthful to who we are by staying inclined to who we belong to. We belong to God as we stay committed to Jesus, and remain faithful in our belief in him fully. The deeper we are in Christ, the deeper awareness we have of ourselves positively and negatively.

The reason we get so upset about how people treat and view us is because we haven't matured in the truth of who we are. Further, we let people treat us how they treat us, and we allow how people view us to affect us because we are not confident in the truth of all that we are. The confident truth of all that we are is found in Jesus Christ. When we arrive in Christ we arrive in truth, and we receive the gift of God- the Holy Spirit who leads us into all truth, including the truth about ourselves.

"The truth makes us free" as it brings closure and disclosure into our lives. Therefore, when we are led by the Holy Spirit into the whole truth of who we are we receive fulfillment. We are fulfilled by the filling of the Holy Spirit which satisfies the void of ignorance of ourselves. This truth allows us to see falsehoods and truths about us from a positive and negative perspective, which allows us to be content with all that God has made and is making us to be.

Intangible

It's human nature to want and have a sense of being in control. This is what has allowed logic and reason to govern humanity in today's society. We exist today in an era where structure, strategy, and statistics are the pillars of truth for mankind. Those factors allow us to make sense out of this life. However, what happens when what makes sense in life plays against us? Further, what happens when what makes sense is devastating and detrimental to our lives?

For some of us in society, structure, strategy, and statistics, places us in areas in society where we don't want to be or cannot stay. For some of us in society, structure, strategy, and statistics keep us doomed. At some point in our lives, I believe we all arrive at a place where we need miracles to happen. Hope is essential for the underdogs of society, and faith is all the structure, strategy, and statistics we need. There are some of us who are hoping and counting on life to not make sense. Why can't life just work out?

We are not satisfied with life just working out because we are so wrapped up in ourselves. In our human nature, we seek satisfaction for fulfillment. But as long as we live, in this mortal life, we will always seek satisfaction. This mortal life is temporary, and each day we live we are on our way to die. Therefore, we seek completion to fulfill various hungers in our humanity.

I like to think this is because it is in our nature to be complete by having a sense of emptiness after fulfillment. It's curious to me that as much as society lives in falsehoods, it is our nature to find truth. We need the truth because the truth fulfills us and keeps us progressing as truth discloses things to us and brings us closure. Truthfully, I believe we fear not knowing the truth. Yet we also even fear knowing the truth, as it frees us. The path to freedom can be a fatal journey if we're not brave enough or open to transparency in receiving the truth.

We have become so fearful in today's society, to the point that even when people do good and nice things for us for no reason, we question it. People have adapted into artificial beings, as we are more like machines computing, assessing, and analyzing everything in life. We're no longer organic beings where we respond and react based on emotion. It is curious how in today's society we are eliminating emotion by conditioning human beings to "not take things personal" but be "professional" or "act appropriately." You see, we're always assessing, analyzing our behavior, we're no longer settled in a relaxed state in our humanity.

This is because fear will cause us to stay on the edge. Fear has always had three faces. Fear shows its face in the beauty of awareness, in the passiveness of concern, and in the aggression of terror. Satan knows that if he can get us to linger in concern, he can keep us in between where he really wants us. Satan really wants us in the shooting range of terror.

As long as terror is staring us in the face, even if we don't clearly see it, we will always be aligned with it in the dark of fear. We are living in the darkness of leaning on our own understanding. Today, if society can't understand something, it wants no part of it. This clouds us from seeing the entire picture that God is really in control. We have become blind to God as we have turned a blind eye to love. Our blindness of God is why we've turned a blind eye to love and have turned ourselves to the false security of our own understanding.

The pursuit of our own understanding comes from our human nature to want to be in control of our own lives and destiny. We are not the author of our own lives, Jesus is because he is the "author of life." As we are not the authors of our own life chronicle, we don't have the right to dictate the truth of who we are and our true purpose. I've found life to hold various purposes for us individually as we continue to live and grow.

As we continue to grow in faith, we will have moments where we are unable to define ourselves and where we're at in life. In fact, I've learned this lesson over and over again until I grasped the reality that our lives have limits when we label its context with definition. Who are we to define any aspects of our lives that God has already proclaimed?

All we need in the moments of our lives where we don't have understanding is to have an understanding of God. God has already defined us, and every aspect of our lives. We don't need to define ourselves. What we are meant to do in life is live according to God's plan for our lives. This makes life a process of refinement and not a practice of living by our own definition.

We have to discipline ourselves to live an intangible life. This is living life depending on Christ, which requires us to walk on water as "we are stewards and ministers on account of the mysteries of God." As disciples of Jesus, we are fishermen of men. Being fishermen of men we are required to operate in stewardship and in ministry on behalf of God's Word.

Living life intangibly is like being still in a flowing river. The current of the waters has its own pace, and the depths of its wonders are deep. Christ is the flowing river, and all we have to do is be still and let the flow of God take us to where He has predestined us to be. This takes having faith.

We have lost sight of what faith is. Faith has no distinct strategy, only our dependency on God's Word. "We are unworthy servants of Christ, and living according to God's Word and our belief in Christ is our duty." There is no payment for having faith, but only grace and mercy that is sufficient. God's love for us is what brings forth what we hope to see beyond what we deserve, and beyond any structure, strategy, or statistic, we can conjure up.

Our love for God by being obedient includes having faith in God, but as we are obedient, we find satisfaction and gain motivation by seeing God's grace and mercy of granting us our hopes, goals, and dreams that seem impossible. This is assurance that cannot be structured, strategized, or governed by statistics, because this is blessed assurance. Blessed assurance is intangible and therefore unable to be broken.

Trailblazing is Walking on Water

If we could never identify who we were and where we were purposed to be, could we keep pressing forward? If we could never experience the comfort of peace, the satisfaction of happiness, or the sustenance of joy, would we choose to still serve God? If God seized promoting us any further, required us to make do with the little we had, and settle with failure and nothing but the success of a lesson, would we even give our lives for Christ with the right heart? These are questions that challenge those born to trail-blaze.

Trailblazing is what I always felt I was meant to do in doing my part in the legacy of Jesus Christ. As God's chosen people, I believe we are designed to trail-blaze the legacy of Jesus Christ because we were sanctified (set apart), and ordained as prophets to the nations to spread the Good News (Gospel) of Jesus. Therefore, promotion and progress may sometimes be difficult to do unless God alone authorizes us to move forward. This is challenging because it requires constant faith in God to make single steps forward, which causes us to walk blind to logic and reason by choice and the understanding and acceptance that God alone is able and will allow us to move forward.

The blessing in surrendering and committing to this lifestyle is that because every step we make is authorized by God, every move we make is blessed. Therefore, if God moves us forward we're blessed. By the same token, if God moves us backward we're still blessed. All things will work together for our good because we are sealed in God's predestined purpose over our lives. It's a frustrating and complicated life at times, and it takes discipline in God's Word to get used to this lifestyle, but because we were chosen, God gives us the strength to endure.

It takes endurance to be a trailblazer in Christ as the life of a trailblazer of God's purpose requires us to walk on water consistently. By this I mean being a trailblazer of God requires living against the odds and becoming accustomed to seeing the impossible fulfilled. The life of a trailblazer of God is a life of a fisherman of men. This means sometimes we are going to have to get wet and sometimes we have to even get soaked, leaving us in cold circumstances in life.

The road of a trailblazer's life is like a river that flows. The current is strong and the waters are deep with God's flow.

This flow does not allow us control and this can be uncomfortable, but as long as we don't fight God's current, we'll end up at the destination where God has appointed us to be.

Our natural desire to want to be in control is what causes us to fight the current, which makes God's flow in our lives more difficult and a much rougher ride. We have to learn to become accustomed to keeping cool in God's current. This takes relying and trusting in God which takes getting to know Him and growing confident in God by remaining still along the way.

Sometimes the hardest thing we can do is be still when we sense the flow of life is moving. We fight the current of God's flow in our lives because we are afraid. We are afraid because we have not been made perfect in love, and we lack the understanding of God's love for us.

We gain understanding of God's love for us as we remain in Christ. We remain in Christ as we continue to believe in him. The belief we have in Jesus is associated with the ear we give to comprehend the Word of God. Comprehending the Word of God ignites our faith in God through our dependence on Jesus Christ. Our belief in Christ allows us to keep the faith to stay on the road and trail-blaze in our walk with God.

If we want to walk with God, we have to walk on water, and sometimes we have to get in the water and get wet. This leaves us soaked in the intangible faith experience with God, leaving on us the residue of our faith walk. Trailblazing in the legacy of Christ requires us to bask in the residue of the journey God has set before us toward the fulfillment of the purpose God predestined for us to arrive in.

Recovering the Inside Truth

Growing up, I can honestly say I've had a great upbringing to which I cannot complain. "No worries that I've ever had can add a single moment to my life," and when we really think about it, no worries ever add to our lives. Even if we are in the midst of trouble and tribulation, worry doesn't add to the moment in time we're in because we're yet living in it.

In spite of every trial I've faced in life, I've learned to "count it all joy" as maturity grooms me to say, "I'm here now, and I have no choice but to go through my situation if I want to get through my situation." It may be difficult to "count it all joy" in the moment, but it's a moment nonetheless, and life still goes on. When we find ourselves in a low place in life we have a habit of remaining in a pity. When our lives seem to be in a "putty" state, we can't afford to have a "pity party." This is the time to focus, and build spiritually.

Our lives are not immune to unfortunate circumstances. There are some of us, unfortunately, who are not very fortunate in specific areas in life. However, we must proceed otherwise. It's a challenge, and it can make life seem to be a bitter sweet experience, but I've learned that there is more than one way we can look at our lives, even in what seems to be negativity.

What is negativity to those God has chosen? Life is not life without the positives and negatives that come with it. It is the negatives and positives of life that make life real; makes life true. Without the positives and negatives of life one cannot proceed in truth.

There is nothing like being victorious, but even greater, there is nothing like being victorious with thorns in our sides. The thorns in our sides on the road to victory keeps us focused for what may come next. For example, death is esteemed as a negative thing, as people view death as the end.

However, death for those chosen in God is not the end, but it is rather a pause for transformation of the being that has been struck with the sting of death- a sting that is unavoidable. It's time for us to learn to brace ourselves for stings in mortal life, because mortal life is full of stings preparing us for the final sting. At some point God has to allow someone, something, or somewhere to take us out. Therefore, it is up to us to be ready to be taken out. The challenge is in this fight to the death called life, will our performance in the fight be tragic or triumphant?

People get so wrapped up in winning and not losing, but what do we do when the outcome of the fight is unanimous even before it begins? Society has it confused. It's not all about the outcome of the fight that determines our victory it's about the performance.

In this mortal life, we are dying, and there is nothing we can do to prevent this outcome. Looking at our mortal lives, in our corrupt bodies, we want to hold on and save ourselves. However, it's not about saving the body. It's all about saving the spirit from destruction. Satan is more concerned with destroying what's intangible on the inside, opposed to what is tangible on the outside.

Satan is destroying people faster in today's society, because he is stealing our integrity in God. He steals our integrity in God by feeding us deceptive truths about ourselves. We then get so wrapped up in the "vision" that we forget about the visionary. The visionary is God. We can be nothing and are nothing without God authorizing us to be so or not to be so. In our ignorance of this truth we "lean to our own understanding" of who we think we are.

When we allow Satan to steal our integrity in God we give him the power to change our identity. This is how hurt people become addicts, misunderstood youth become juvenile offenders, and lost people end up committing suicide. When we allow Satan to steal our integrity in God we give him possession of the core of who we are.

If Satan possesses the core of who we are, he then has the possession over the essence of who we are. This is what I believe being possessed really is in common cases. Crawling up walls because we're possessed is a worse-case scenario, but we are not too far from this as long as Satan has possession of the core essence of our minds.

As Satan has possession of our core essence he gains the ability to alter our true identity. Satan cannot create but he is a master manipulator. Therefore, when we allow Satan to get so far that he has the power to alter our identity we start to seek after ourselves. This is what Satan wants because to seek after ourselves is a character trait of his own.

Seeking after ourselves is not a character trait of Jesus, as Christ only sought after God the Father's will. Therefore, our character identifies more toward the image and likeness of Satan's if we are "depending on our own understanding of ourselves". The more we seek after ourselves the more we are seeking after our own corrupt nature which is fused with sin nature.

As we seek ourselves further, we forsake our fear of God, and meet with the evil that we are. Seeking ourselves leads to the same route of the sin nature that exists within us. The pursuit of ourselves by depending on our own understanding is forsaking our fear of God because of our disobedience of God's Word which tells us "not to depend on our own understanding." The Bible tells us, "Trust in the LORD with all your heart; do not depend on your own understanding. Seek his will in all you do, and he will show you which path to take. Don't be impressed with your own wisdom. Instead, fear the LORD and turn away from evil."

With Satan's ability to alter our identity, we become his puppets. As puppets of Satan, we become subject to how he wants to dress us. As a result, our image is now subject to becoming defiled or defaced over time. We see this image with people who live a lifestyle of drug abuse. They began to look bad from all the drug use. We see this image with people who have "sold their soul" for the love of money. They may look very good but their demeanor is very ugly. All this happens because we fail to remain true to who we are and more so who we belong to.

However, there is still hope to recover ourselves by repenting and coming to Jesus. There is nothing that Christ can't heal. Christ can even raise us from the dead that we are inside ourselves, and I believe this is what most of us need. We need to be revived in Christ in order to recover.

We limit recovery to addicts but we all are guilty (to some degree) of being addicted to our very selves. At least people addicted to drugs, alcohol, sex, or other substances, can easily identify and extract what the problem is. We can get a handle on our-self by seeking and holding on to the Word of God. We must recover who we are in Christ to bask in who God created us to be through Christ. It is who God created us to be through Christ that lets us know we are in alignment with the truth of who we are.

Recovery is a process of spiritual rejuvenation toward spiritual restoration. Some of us are so lost in ourselves and have allowed Satan to shatter our identity to the point that the pieces cannot be put back together: We need total "newness." Christ makes all things new and we can be made new in him. One can never fully know the depth of who they are until they arrive in the fullness of God's glory in Heaven. Imagine how much more we really are in Christ: This is our hope that we will recover who we are. We are more than what life or ourselves could ever ask or think to be.

~ Chapter Twelve ~

Wholeness

Lord, Where do I Fit

I am who God says I am. I cannot be defined by my own understanding, and not even by anyone else's. As we are beings subject to time, we are subject to change.

It's human nature to define oneself. We don't like to feel lost. Feeling lost in one's self is one of the most depressing feelings anyone can have. It's like a living nightmare when you don't feel present in your own skin. Some of us are just here! At that point, we are where we are, and we are waiting to be pulled out of wherever we are.

Honestly, I have never really felt secure in many settings. Home is where the heart is and my heart has not been in many things, although my attitude may have fooled many. While I've always seemed to fit in with various people the fit was never secure.

The fit was always too tight or too loose. In neither fit did I find comfort in what I seemed to be compatible with. This taught me that while people can seem to belong, the truth of confidently knowing that you belong is the true sense of feeling at home.

Some of us are in the wrong place in the right "puzzle." If this is the case, it may be that God has to take the time to mold us into where He wants us to fit. I haven't been in many positions where all of me honestly fit in, or even wanted to fit in. I can only think of a few.

One example is my relationship, with my fiancée. I've always felt like all of me fit in our relationship. However, there were times where God had to pull us apart, which left me feeling out of place. There are times when you find a place where you are sure that you fit, and God will pull you away from that. Naturally, in response, we get angry at God because we feel denied of the comfort we've found. When this happens we have to trust God.

Sometimes God will separate us from a person, place, or thing because we've become more attached to it more than we are attached to Him. The separation can be temporarily or permanently. It's alright to be secure in the fit we find, but we must not get stuck on the satisfaction of the fit.

Getting stuck on the satisfaction of the fit can make the fit an idol before God, which He does not desire. God knows when we get too comfortable in the fit and will not allow the comfort to deviate us from our destiny in Him. He loves us to much to let this happen.

God is not going to allow us to be secure in anyone not secure in Him. We cannot be so secure in the nouns of life because we must be able to function in God with or without them. Jesus alone is who completes us.

We have to be unmovable in God so if even what we love most moves or is moved, we'll remain secure. This is not just for our sake, but for their sake as well. We are not to be unequally yoked under any circumstances. God taught me to never allow myself to be too secure in anything subject to time because anything subject to time can crumble.

Therefore, don't be so attached to substances that can be broken by the weathering of time. Attaching ourselves to these substances can yoke us so well that when they break we become broken too because we're yoked to them.

Now this is not speaking against oneness, but it is rather for oneness. If we are to operate in the full strength and power of oneness, we must be whole individually so collectively we can continue to stand whenever others fall. By remaining whole as an individual, we can help pick up those who have been broken that we are connected to. One is not truly whole separated from Jesus Christ.

In essence, if we want to be one, we have to get on one accord with the Holy Spirit. It is the Holy Spirit who is the gift of God that "leads us into all truth". Truth again, discloses and brings closure. This leaves us whole as truth grants us the satisfaction of fulfillment- security.

It is very difficult to be whole without security. Many people are unsatisfied and therefore they feel insecure. They search for satisfaction in people, places, and things all to find themselves disappointed as time goes by if not immediately. Satisfaction in people, place, and things do not last. Eventually, the satisfaction will run out. We need an eternal supply.

In Jesus we have satisfaction and find security, and we are unmovable and yet mobile. In Christ there is true freedom.

Dare to be Unusual

Check this thought out: Everyone in this world has an origin, a story, and a legacy. Jesus Christ is the author of the chronicle of our lives. I call life a chronicle because I see it as bigger than a single story. The life we live is our story, but I have learned that a life story is always connected to the legacy of a person. A legacy brings the origin of a story into being.

The story of a persons' life is like a wrapped blanket in time sealed between two knots tied on both ends. Our life stories are connected with others in this exemplified manner. Every life story starts with a sealed knot and ends with a sealed knot. The blanket wrapped contains all the content of our lives.

Some people choose to write their own story, but this is essentially impossible. Ultimately, God writes our story through Jesus Christ, and we all have a role to play. We can try to live as free agents by living how we want to live, as most people do, but in reality, it is inevitable not to play out our role on God's stage. However, many people play the roles they desire, and in this they are living off script; altering their life story, and in turn, defiling the story God has already written concerning them.

Living life is all about how we carry ourselves. How we carry ourselves is all about the character we display. We are who we are but the essential truth of who we are is based upon who we belong to. We either belong to Christ or we belong to Satan. In reality there is no in-between: no gray area.

To get to the meat of this section, I've learned there is no need wasting time to change somebody. I've found that when we want things to change we should be the factor that changes in the situation. As a result, we experience change in our situation because we were the factor in the situation that changed. Therefore, we caused the situation to change.

Everybody wants change, but everybody is afraid of change. We look around at one another dumbfounded, waiting on other factors to change, when in actuality, we are the only ones who can be sure we want change. Fear predominantly is what prevents change from occurring. We are so afraid to dare to be unusual, and yet we want unusual things to happen for us in our lives.

If we want to see odd things happen to us, we have to sometimes be brave enough to stand out as the odd man out.

We have to dare to be unusual. This takes a willingness to accept persecution, ridicule, and looking like a fool for a period of time. Jesus Christ dared to be unusual by doing God's will.

To this day, Christ is still being persecuted by the persecution that unbelievers inflict on those who believe in him (Acts 9:1-4). Yes, being a disciple of Jesus is daring to be unusual. In fact, standing out among other believers can take daring to be unusual.

"Dare to be unusual!" This statement said to me by Reverend Dwayne Wilkins revolutionized my perspective on life during my teenage years. I heard this at a youth service at my church at the time: Tasker Street Missionary Baptist Church. It encouraged me to be myself, and so I did, due to the impact these words had on my life. God used this statement to lift me out of a suicidal and depressed state that was really heavy on me at the time.

It wasn't easy either. I had to think on this statement almost every second of the day until I started feeling better. Sometimes I have to remember these words even now.

Daring to be unusual isn't meant to be easy. It is meant to refine how we view ourselves and live. It requires stepping out on the faith of who we are in Christ and finding security in this.

It takes a lot to stand out as you, because you are one of a kind. Don't you know that there's nobody in the world that is the same as you are? Everybody is "fearfully and wonderfully" made, and we are made in the uniqueness God desired to make us.

The enemy doesn't want us to see who we really are. If we were able to see the fullness of who we really are life probably would not have as much weight as it does because this would make us secure or prompt us to change. So Satan puts things in place to keep us from seeing who we are by blocking us from seeing what God wants us to see about us. God wants us to see ourselves through the mirror of His Word.

Jesus Christ and the Word are one in the same. If we can only learn to keep our focus on Christ, we can see who we really are. I don't know if God can let us see the fullness of who we are at once. We are not likely ready to receive certain things about us from God. So acceptance is the roadblock in this case. This shows us that the problem with daring to be unusual really comes from within us.

In going through whatever we must go through with God, we must learn patience and have faith to dare to be unusual enough that we are who He says we are. We learn who we are by looking in God's mirror. God's mirror is His Word.

The reason we fail to get even a glimpse of the truth of who we are is because we fail to open our Bibles and observe ourselves through the Word of God. Now when I say observe, I don't mean just reading with your eyes, but seeing, perceiving, and receiving with your heart through the conviction of the Holy Spirit. We need to come to understand God for who He is in His Word so that we can get a true glimpse of who we are.

However, this is all impossible without the Holy Spirit leading us. It's the Holy Spirit that compels us ahead of ourselves to seek God and come to an understanding of who God is. For example, Christ asked his disciples who they thought he was, Peter responded, "You are the Son of God-the Messiah." In response, Christ told Peter, "You could not have known this on your own, and that it was the Spirit who revealed this to him." That same Spirit that revealed the true identity of Jesus Christ to Peter is the Holy Spirit who reveals to us not only Christ, but leads us to the truth about who we really are in Christ.

We have to dare! Be daring enough to seek God, and by the "push" of the Holy Spirit, allow ourselves to receive the truth, especially the truth about ourselves. Can we really be brave enough to step out of our comfortable understanding of who we think we are, and step out on faith and gain understanding to come to know who we really are?

This is a challenge that can shake up our lives, but will refine us in confidence if we allow it. However, first, we must stand up and dare to be unusual enough to lose ourselves in order to find the truth. We strive to be daring enough to find the truth of who we are to break down barriers in our society.

People are afraid to be who they really are because very few other people are being who they really are. This is a form of spiritual warfare that everyone can see but no one wants to admit. For one to admit that one has barriers up regarding who they are, this would disclose the truth that fear by way of insecurity exist in that individual. Lowering the barriers of who we are leaves us open.

The first step in breaking down barriers among one another is by revealing the truth that there are barriers.

Second, in order to literally break down barriers, someone amid this spiritual stand still must let down their barriers. We must allow ourselves to be open if we expect others to be open to us. This is a key component that the church must master.

It's not about being honest to hurt someone's feelings. It's about being sincere with people so that true progress can be made in that person, our self, and society. Everyone has good and bad things about them.

The Gift within the Gift

People are like Styrofoam cups. We come in packs and we are easily blown away in the strong winds that blow our way if were empty. If we were to leave an empty cup outside on a windy day, it would easily blow away. However, if you fill it with a substance that the cup is designed to carry anyway, it obtains the weight it needs to stand despite the winds that blow.

People need satisfaction and security. The proper satisfaction and the proper security is what fills us, and rather, fulfills us to live on and stand in adversity. Adversity can be very real. Sometimes it can almost seem as though the winds of adversity is directly blowing at us as if it is designed specifically to knock us down. However, we must stand and remain in position because our adversity is indeed designed to take us out, along with those connected to us.

We are a body, a pyramid of cups, and at the top of the pyramid is the cup that pours into us all. That cup is Jesus Christ, and what we receive into us is the Holy Spirit. The Holy Spirit is the living water that we receive from God after receiving Jesus as our Lord and Savior.

As God has poured His Spirit into Christ, who stands at the top of the pyramid of his chosen, the Spirit overflows out of Christ, and as he has received the overflow of the Holy Spirit, we receive the overflow of God's Spirit streaming out of Christ into us. We receive the outpouring of the Holy Spirit and out of us also flows rivers of living water that pours out into others as we remain in alignment with Christ.

We have to stay aligned with Christ if we want to continue to receive the outpouring of the Holy Spirit. Sometimes we take ourselves out of alignment of Christ. This disconnects us from the pyramid which prevents us from receiving the outpouring of God's Spirit. In a domino effect, we affect those connected to us from receiving what we should be receiving to share.

This is exactly what many people do: we get our portion from the Spirit and keep it for ourselves. As a result, we no longer receive fresh dosages of the outpouring of gifts, and we are left with what we have received. That's a good lesson that God allows us to learn. He sometimes allows us to keep what we receive, and after a while the living water we received evaporates or is used up after we pour it into whom, what, or where we choose to invest the gift in.

It is not up to us to keep or invest the gifts of the Holy Spirit that God has given us as we choose. It is up to us to stay in place and stay connected to God through Christ. We do this so that we can continue to receive what God has given Christ. By staying connected to Christ we continue to receive the gifts of the Holy Spirit, and we can be used to share it with those who Christ has chosen.

So often, we get caught up in the gifts we receive in the gift. However, it is all about the gift that empowers the gift. The gift that empowers our gift is the gift of the Holy Spirit. The Holy Spirit is the gift within the gift that keeps on giving.

The potency of the gifts we receive has not much to do with how we dress it up. It doesn't even depend on how we groom it, because some of us groom the gifts we have received amiss. We nurture our gifts in and with the wrong things: perverting our gifts.

We strengthen our gifts with the Word of God and by using them as they are meant to be used. Many people prostitute their gifts by putting a price tag on it. Now we all must make a living, and it is a blessing to be able to use our gifts in conjunction of how we make a living. However, as our gifts are given freely, we have to make use of them freely.

It is important for us to make room to present our gifts in acts of charity, and not allow them to be available only for cash. As God gives us the gift of the Holy Spirit as an act of love freely we should remember to give it freely to others in love.

Without the gift of the Holy Spirit filling us we are empty. Being empty spiritually is the same as being incomplete. We remain incomplete when we are void of Christ in our lives. Sure, we find substitutes such as academia, religion, money, sex, etcetera to fill the emptiness, but these substitutes always leave us continuing to chase for more substitutes.

We continue to chase because nothing man made or objective to the will of God can fulfill us. We need fulfillment to satisfy our desire of living a full life. However, it isn't what we receive that fulfills us, it is actually our release of what we receive that fulfills us.

I am a man who hungers and thirst for fulfillment. I've been nourished and satisfied, but I've learned by looking at myself and others, that as long as we have breath in our bodies, we will always seek satisfaction. However, satisfaction in Christ is not like man driven satisfaction. Satisfaction in Christ continues as we grow from faith to faith and glory to glory.

The more we receive from Christ the more we are supposed to give. The more we give as we're connected to Christ, the more we will continue to receive. This applies for those who are living in Christ as well as those who have died in Christ. In life or death, as long as we are connected to Christ, rivers of living water flow out of us. It's a spiritual gift not a physical gift; although, the gift can manifest in the physical.

It's all about completion from this life to the next. Don't die undone! Don't live or die without obtaining a relationship with Jesus. Do you know him? The gift within the gift that empowers the gift God gives us, gives from generation to generation.

~ Chapter Thirteen ~

PONDERING "MASA" AT THE PEAK

Facing off with America

First off, I want to make it clear before I begin that I love the country I live in. America to me is home, and despite what I perceive and what is the truth of this country, America, in my opinion, is the best country to live on Earth. That being said, the truth is the truth, the truth will make us free, and I believe that the truth has a place and time to be spoken. Therefore, since I'm writing this book, which allows me the privilege to express my thoughts freely, I want to speak out further about the dynamics I see regarding the heart, the soul, and the mind of America.

When I speak of the heart, the mind, and the soul of America, I'm referring to America's spirit. When I speak of the spirit of America, I'm talking about the character of America. This includes the integrity, identity, and image of America: the spiritual, mental, and physical face of the United States.

The face of this country is hidden. We the people, hide our faces under a mask of make-up. The make-up that we dress our true face in consists of the illusion of confidence, truth, and reverence for God.

All these illusions are the make-up one needs to make one-self appear secure, sincere, and sanctified by God. It has always been America's foolish desire to be divine and not walk truthfully in the grace and mercy of God. We are blessed that God has not consumed us concerning all we have done and still do.

For centuries we have claimed to know God, but we just know of Him. In our ignorance, we ignore God's truth, and therefore, we fail to be truthfully Godly. Despite all our years that we have proclaimed "In God We Trust," we have failed to know intimately who God is for ourselves. The Christianity we claim is nothing but a shadow of the Roman Empire.

Remaining in our bold ignorance of God and our foolish refusal to acknowledge God truthfully, we dare not show our face bare. We must wear the make-up we have worn for centuries- the make-up of a false confidence, a false truth, and our false reverence of God.

Like the great nation of Ancient Rome before us, whom we model and admire, we bare destruction on our foreheads because we have seen the truth of God and yet we have chosen to not believe. This is our greatest offense that we have made before God, as for anyone else who makes this offense. For anyone who has seen the truth of God, and has the residue of being blessed reeking from their being, and chooses to still deny the Son of God, this is a major offense that should not be difficult to understand.

To note, accepting only ninety-nine percent of the doctrine of Jesus Christ is still rejecting him one hundred percent. God continues to bless us, yet we have the audacity to continue to reject Him and the gift He has given and claim the effect of the gift within the gift He has given us as something that comes from us.

One of the biggest problems in America in regard to God is that God is not a commitment in this country. God is only convenient in this country. In fact, the only time we want to acknowledge God or anything spiritual is when it is obvious we don't have an answer. Further, we acknowledge God when the nation is in trouble, or wants to justify its pursuit of justice.

God and His Word (the Bible/the Canon) is only convenient in this nation when we want to justify ourselves in an illogical position. We foolishly insult God by acting as if He is blind to the truth that pertains to us. However, there is no truth or falsehood that God cannot see. God is the light that shines through any darkness. His light cannot and will not be extinguished.

The spirit of this nation is as black as the pigmentation that this country hates. There is a mystery behind this. "Masa" will never allow us to truly see ourselves as the light of this world. Therefore, "Masa" has to corrupt the mind, enslave the body, and oppress the spirit of who we are.

This does not apply to white people alone; this applies to everyone who carries this "Masa" spirit. People who carry this kind of spirit of oppression show it in the way they think. They ignore the obvious negative truth, and they avoid the truth that something must be done to make change by downplaying that an issue is a "big deal" or if an issue really exist.

Sadly, black folk point the finger at white folk, but of a truth I see black folk carrying the "Masa" spirit as well. "Masa" is nothing but a persona of ignorance not willing to change; a thug mentality; a persona of Satan. The only difference is that the "Masa" persona is one of the weakest and most cowardly personas the enemy has. This is because the persona of the "Masa" spirit is straightforward and obvious in its ignorance.

Ignorance is one of this country's most common and obvious imperfections. The shame of this truth is that even every nation outside of America can see this. While other nations can have some evil traits about them as well, they are true to their cause and very open with the truth of their ways.

I don't agree with some other countries either, but it's simpler to have to deal with a devil you know than to deal with a devil you don't know. I've learned to appreciate a demon who is truthful in that it is demonic than a demon who dresses himself in the deception of holiness.

We deceive others and ourselves in the persona of holiness that is easily disproven among American citizens when we consider the love we have among one another.

America lacks in love and is held hostage in fear. Fear engulfs this nation inside and out. Ever since 9/11 we remain guarded.

This has grown worse and worse, as we aren't just guarded toward other nations, but toward one another. The fear that engulfs this country proves we are not perfect in love and that in God we actually do not trust. We fall short of the glory of God by default anyhow, because everyone does, and even further, because we linger in our shortcoming of God's glory as we have chosen to lean on the sweet deception of our own voice to define ourselves.

If any nation has become lost in the refinement of God it is the United States of America because we thrive upon the definition we have given ourselves. Our entire nation is built on a false identity of a people that defines its self as a nation built on Christian principles. I find this to be false.

Our nation was not built on Christian principles but on Christian practice. The practice of Christianity softens our hard reputation. There is a thin line between practice and principle. Practice is the application of a custom and teaching. Principle is the comprehension of a belief or doctrine.

By this I can conclude that America's relationship with God is not solid. One's relationship with God cannot be solidified based upon intellect of God alone. One's relationship with God is solidified based upon intimacy in God. Therefore, if we ever want to be a country built on Christian principles in secure confidence, sincere truth, and in sanctified reverential fear of God, demolition, uprooting, and reconstruction, must take place at ground zero.

We must become a refined nation in God. Then we will truly be "one nation under God, indivisible," and we will finally see "liberty and justice for all." However, refinement in God must take place or this will not happen. We cannot be refined until we truthfully receive Jesus Christ in the fullness of who he is in accordance to the Word of God, and remain in him. Then we will see how truly beautiful America can be.

Reaffirming the Truth

African Americans are losing their faith in God and their belief in Jesus Christ in the fullness of his identity according to the Bible more and more. Our allegiance to God through Christ has been shaken by the anger of the remnants of our past struggles still present in this country. Further, the temperature of our sensitivity to the Holy Spirit, as our keeper, has become cold by the heat of our success.

Despite the many opinions that African Americans share a common ground upon, the fact that is evident is that we have made progress. Although many may have counted us out in this country, and throughout the world, God, by His Spirit, has not let us down. However, many disagree, and this attitude has led me to speak up. Plain and simple, God has never let us down. We chose to no longer lift Him up in our lives individually and as a people united.

No one may have noticed, but more and more, I see the soul of my people depleting. As time rolls by, we are becoming a people that we are not. Now there are some things that we cannot change about ourselves, because God willed us to be a certain way. However, what we cannot change, we can alter. For example, you can teach a dog how to speak on command, but the dog will always have his own tone in his bark.

All we can do is sensitize or desensitize people when we want to alter what we cannot change. A black man in America is still a man in America. The only thing that alters the fact that a man is a black man in America is the emphasis we place behind the fact. We must be watchful of emphasis we place behind facts. The emphasis we place behind facts has the ability to either sensitize or desensitize the truth of the facts.

This is what society has done to the black race. What makes this an evil act aside from the fact that no one should alter anyone to a false truth, is that society has desensitized society to position black folk at a position where they are always under control. The hard truth I see in society is that African Americans and black people in general, in today's society, remain puppets even when we think we have been placed in a position of freedom or leadership.

As we give in to believing that we are in control we relinquish our true position of freedom. It's sad that with all the marching, all the suffering, all the positive sensitizing we've done in this country to be free, we yet remain slaves-enslaved by our mentality of what freedom is. Freedom is living unbound, but even in living we are bound to life itself. The only true and real freedom is freedom through Jesus Christ as our Lord and Savior.

Christ is the only freedom we ever had in this country. It was never in financial stability, career choice, equality, or realized dreams. As long as we keep looking at each other to define what freedom looks like, we will always be enslaved. It's curious how we've looked at white folk and labeled them the face of freedom. As a result from this, we formed a definition of what it means to be free based on the persona of what we identify freedom to look like.

However, now, in consideration of black college graduates who we consider by default, our leaders and success stories, the truth is coming to the light that the success of the educated and financially progressed African American is not freedom. I say this based upon my experience as well as others I know who are college graduates and have made advancements in their finances due to their education. We played the game to be free, and we acquired the qualifications to be free, but we still don't feel free. This is because we are not free by these things alone.

We have sensitized ourselves to what freedom is supposed to look like, and yet we still lack in our sense of freedom. We lack in our sense of freedom, simply because we are not free in our minds. Now, if we played the game [mentally] to be free, and we acquired the qualifications [physically] to be free, why is it that we still do not feel free? It's not that we are ignorant to what freedom is by human definition.

Here lies our mistake because of our misinterpretation. We make the mistake of what freedom is because our definition of freedom is not what freedom truly is. Freedom is nothing tangible and it cannot be obtained physically, but it can be obtained mentally, from either a physical or spiritual perspective. It all depends upon what causes the person to experience and feel free.

Therefore, if we feel free because of the physical factors that influence our lives that are causing us to perceive we are free, then by this perception we are free. By the same token, if we feel free because of spiritual facts that influence our lives that are causing us to perceive we are free, then by this perception we are free. However, spiritual freedom and physical freedom are different.

Physical freedom is temporary and is liable to what is natural. Spiritual freedom is eternal and is liable to what is spiritual. It all depends upon the person's perception and choice of what is freedom. However, we must consider if freedom is really freedom when it is liable? Does freedom have a cost? Freedom indeed has a cost, but the cost was paid with the sacrifice of Jesus Christ on the cross. True freedoms' cost was paid on the cross, and Christ purchased it.

To my discovery, I've found that as long as we live and as long as we exist we will always be slaves. However, the problem is not the enslavement. The problem is the enslaver. It all depends on who or what we are slaves to.

We are all slaves. We are either slaves to ourselves, slaves to our careers, slaves to money, slaves to academia, or slaves to others. We can even be slaves to visions, dreams, and goals. Some people are even slaves to fear, jealousy, and pride. However, I pose to us that it is better to be a slave to Christ because it is through him that we were made.

Being a slave to Christ is being a slave to truth. When we are slaves to Jesus Christ we are home and we have freedom, because in Christ is the source of all that we are. Satan used "Masa" to deceive us into thinking that Christ belonged to them when "Masa" was the one subject to Christ and he didn't even belong to Christ because his character was always contrary to the Word of God, even as a master.

We got caught up in "Masa" enslaving us and teaching us the Bible, perverting the Word in the heart of his teachings to confuse us to corruption and increase his superiority. Yet, while our physically enslaved ancestors of the past were wise enough to recognize the deception, we, being physically free men of the present, are foolish enough to be deceived. Satan was smart enough to know that he couldn't keep some of us bound physically in time as time progressed. God would not allow this. However, Satan was cunning enough to use "Masa" to bind us spiritually in the present by the effectual remnants of our past.

The Bible tells us to "not sin while angry," but we let our justified anger cause us to sin against God with the worse sin of all. That sin is our rejection of the truth that Jesus Christ is the Son of God, is God, and that through Christ alone, we have eternal life- salvation. However, we chose to not believe based on Satan's deception of what "Masa" acknowledged as justice, where in actuality, the injustice was in the twisting of the justice. Satan used "Masa" to present the truth to birth our lean on a lie based upon our passion, knowing our passion was what best defined us by human definition.

Once again we stray away from God because we are always leaning on definition and striving to define ourselves. We must do what our ancestors did, and "trust in God with all our heart, not leaning to our own understanding." No matter how bad the situation looks we must trust God. It doesn't matter how much we think we can endure, what matters is God, who gives us the ability, and has given us the ability to endure.

If we question God, and who we are, look at the strength of our peoples' spirit. For centuries, even up to this day, society has strived to break our spirit- the spirit God gave us. However, through it all, our spirit remains intact, and strong, but it is fractured now, because we have disconnected from God- "the joy and the strength of our lives who moves all our pain, misery, and strife."

We must remember who God is. Like the song's lyrics, "we got too fast and pray, stay in the narrow way; keep our life clean every day." God is our all in all! We must remember! Never forget that it was "God of our weary years, God of our silent tears, God who has brought us thus far along the way." We must remember to stay "true to our God till victory is won." Our victory is in our reaffirmation and in our reestablished relationship and allegiance to God through our reverential fear of Him through our belief in Jesus Christ, who is the Son of God, is God, our Lord and Savior, and the holder of our now and eternal salvation.

Acknowledgements

First, I thank God, my Lord and Savior Jesus Christ, and my best friend the Holy Ghost for entrusting me to write these words and pushing me to complete it to the end. I was honestly pretty discouraged throughout the process of completing this project, and God would not let me rest until I finished. I give God the glory for allowing me to know that He put more in me to share.

I also want to thank my first lady, my mom, Gail Stewart. Mom, thank you for allowing God to use you to encourage me to complete this work anyhow despite how big or small it may or may not be. I love you so much. I will never forget all the nights we sat reading over the book aloud and the truthful input you gave that wasn't always easy to swallow.

I also want to thank my wife, Hana Stewart, for putting up with me in my moods and frustration with my writings. Thank you gorgeous, for being understanding during the late nights of writing and respecting my intimate time with

God while He produced these words through me. I Love You always and forever!

I also want to thank my sister, Shira King for talking me out of ceasing to write and to continue on to write it the way God has given the words to me. You know I love you too girl!

Special thanks to Associate Pastor of Kingdom Worship Center Church, Doug Harris. Thank you good sir for your consistent encouragement and enriching advice. Honorable mention to Pastor Damian Stewart (KWCC). I'm still writing cuz!

God Bless you all!

About the Author

Shalom J Stewart, South Philadelphia Native and Graduate of Cheyney University of Pennsylvania. In the spring of 2011, Shalom earned a baccalaureate in Psychology in which has been keynote to his profession. Shalom is passionate about sharing his growth in the knowledge of Jesus Christ in which he believes he is gifted enough to exhort and provide education of his learnings to others. Currently, Shalom attends the Redeemer Institute of Christian Education, A Bible institution under the Evangelical Training Association. He is also the author of ***"Intangible Intimacy: The Diary of a King David Admirer."*** Other projects from the author are soon to come! Email Shalom at **info@stewart.shalom.com** for workshops or other events and information. You can also visit Shalom at his website at **www.shalomjstewart.com**

www.ingramcontent.com/pod-product-compliance
Lightning Source LLC
Chambersburg PA
CBHW051723040426
42447CB00008B/949
* 9 7 8 0 6 9 2 7 0 7 1 1 1 *